Modern Bait
and
Fly   Casting

Second Movement in Bait Casting

MODERN BAIT
AND
FLY CASTING

BY

OZARK RIPLEY

D. Appleton & Company
New York   ::   London
Mcmxxviii

INTRODUCTION

The object of this book is to impart information to anglers in a simple, understandable way, so that they may learn readily to master the proper form of modern bait and fly casting, and apply it to practical fishing at the very first opportunity. What scientific angling has developed is plainly told, instead of the many debatable details and arguments on methods and subjects for which the average man in possession of a vacation period has no time.

THE AUTHOR.

CONTENTS

ix

CONTENTS

ILLUSTRATIONS

PART I
BAIT CASTING

CHAPTER I

THE SPORT OF BAIT CASTING

AFTER a careful survey it is quite easy to see the reason that bait casting has quickly developed into one of the great fishing sports, particularly if we measure the sport by the number of devotees. There seems to be no class of anglers for such fish as pike, muskellunge, and bass, who, however much they are in love with fly casting, do not at some time show considerable activity with the short rod. Strange, too, in late years when brook, rainbow, brown and other species of trout run very large, even the tyro notices that bait casting is featured in the taking of these wonderful sporting fish.

It seems strange that years ago anglers did not devote more attention to bait casting for large trout. Perhaps the cause of it was the firm belief that any of the lures which are used in the sport of bait casting would certainly frighten fish, instead of attracting their attention. Yet, the reverse is often the case. Frequently I have seen brook trout weighing over six pounds quickly seize an unseemly looking artificial bait when the most skilled efforts of great dry fly anglers with tiny small flies, which were regarded as exact replicas of the insects upon which trout feed, failed to be accorded the slightest recognition.

Even on the famed Nipigon, where brook trout grow larger than in any stream on the American continent, repeatedly I have caught with artificial baits made of wood, nickeled iron, spinners, and combinations of feathers, exceedingly big redspots, though previously all my fly-casting artistry had been in vain.

In early days of artificial bass angling those who went in for this noted game fish with flies discovered they had a penchant for striking wickedly at their prey, whether it consisted of frogs, minnows, tadpoles, young birds, moles, or anything which demanded speed on their part for the capture. Moreover, they must have noticed that they smash wickedly at inanimate things that often come their way. When an angler sees a fish rise immediately he will exert himself in almost every imaginable fashion to take it in a sportsmanlike manner. But before making the attempt he invariably asks himself what was the object the

4

fish seized, or for which it rose, and then goes on to contrive something similar.

The trail blazers of bait casting are said to have originated in the state of Kentucky. Those who try to refute this claim immediately find themselves confronted with the facts that the first really good bait-casting reels were manufactured in that state, and so skillfully that some of the original reels made by these early masters compare in execution with any of those of the present, and that the ideas incorporated in them have been pursued almost meticulously by most of the makers of present-day bait-casting reels.

From what we are able to discover by reading and going back into the mountain countries where bass fishing with flies was regarded seriously a long time ago, we find that not only regular bass flies were used, but also artificial minnows were esteemed as great killers. Spinning baits of the old Devon type had their adherents. The artificial minnows were what is known as the phantom; when either these, or any revolving lure were fished with, the sport approximated almost in every way what is known among English anglers as spinning.

Put yourself in the same position as the anglers

5

on the clear mountain streams when the bass was first pursued with their fly rods. At times the clarity of the water, particularly when it was low, was remarkable. The anglers learned then that bass were wary to the limit of wariness, and, no matter how far they could cast a fly with a regular fly rod or fly rod used for spinning baits, it would add much more to their sport if they could get their deceit out a little farther. With a fly rod they attained a certain distance, and this could not be exceeded, though they strove ever so much.

Perhaps the next thing which came to the mind of these anglers was a method of casting lures. They began by casting from the hand, with a long line coiled loosely at their feet. The instant the lure touched the water, if the lure was retrieved by hand, it had the desired action; and, in consequence, many nice fish were taken which would have otherwise been denied them. These anglers found that by the addition of a little weight to their lure they could augment their casting distance.

Two things in the casting game of this sort doubtless encouraged fast thinking. Much would be added to the sport if they could find a rod of suitable length for flinging their lures better than they could with a fly rod. Also if they had a different reel from the regular single-action fly reel, it would not only assist in casting but also expedite in recovering the line. It was a slow task to reel a lot of line with a fly reel; and those which they used could not accommodate the amount of line necessary for casting any good distance, for the art of making the plain silk lines of great strength for fly casting was totally unknown. The first lines were enameled fly lines or ordinary linen lines; the latter became swollen very fast on account of their fondness for soaking up much water, and, therefore, occupied a great amount of room on the spool of the reels.

The changes in rods for the purpose of bait casting were first manifested in the appearance of the reel seat above the hand instead of below the hand; also, the rods were shortened. What then was regarded as an exceedingly short rod was generally eight and a half feet in length, and built with much less whippy action than the regular fly-casting models. The reels developed into the multiplying type; that is, they operated so that the spool revolved from two to four times while the crank was turned once.

7

Naturally one cannot help referring to the early bait-casting reels and marveling at their sturdiness, simplicity, and general utility. Their makers could not have lavished such pains on them had they not been expert anglers; at the same time we must recall that anglers cast live bait with their rods, such as frogs, minnows, cray-fish, etc., as much as, if not more so than, artificial images closely resembling them. Even what then and now are known as still fishermen quickly took up the new type of rods and reels. They were a wonderful improvement over the fly rods or any sort of strip casting.

Many who observed the early pioneers in the bait-casting game were a bit puzzled for an actual estimate of the sport. They were of the same mind as the old dyed-in-the-wool, almost lifetime fly caster when he sees for the first time a man casting an artificial lure. They declared it was a crude, hardly sportsmanlike pastime for taking game fish, and lacked all the delicate art of fly casting. Moreover, they did not recognize it as ethical, but were unanimous in expressing their opinion that it was very bourgeois and never demanded the skill of wrist and study which in their minds they thought fly casting did. The instant

8

they tried their hands at bait casting, invariably they were surprised at their gaucheness and how long it continued, and before many hours they were aware that it required a longer time to become really experienced in bait casting than when they mastered the fly rod; also, under many conditions the sport was on as high a scale, if not higher, provided the right light tackle was featured in fishing.

After bait casting really attained popularity further changes in rods were seen. They became still shorter—even to three and a half feet—because the fishermen who used them declared they were more efficient for casting from along brushy banks and in a boat. Instead of being made from the old standard materials, lancewood, Bethabara, bamboo, and hickory, a useful steel rod at a small price found its way on the market in all lengths.

Few appreciate what the coming of the steel rod did for bait casting. Probably it did more toward recruiting followers of the game than anything else. The cheap price of some steel rods made it convenient for people of the most modest means to own one that was really serviceable. In addition progressive bait-casting ideas were incorporated in them, which even the best makers of high quality bamboo rods soon had to emulate.

Right away the silk line came in vogue. It cast freely, was of finer size, for its strength, than any other line, and very soon showed that it was the only kind which ought to be used for the sport. It caused the changing of patterns for guides and tip tops. These were made larger, so that the line went out without encountering trouble, as when it ran through a tiny aperture. But the friction was so great it cut quickly all old types of steel guides so that at first ones of exceedingly hard steel or metal alloys supplanted them; later agates and imitation agates, as well as those of tungsten, prevented this efficiently and for the life of the rod, and even longer.

Bait casting gained strides with such rapidity that it amazed even the early anglers who predicted a considerable following for it. It became the sport of the masses, not so much because of its cheapness—which must not be regarded as negligible—but because it was a superior way of taking fish without having to go to the trouble of seining live minnows, catching frogs and crawfish, or resorting to the laborious task of digging for the universally popular wriggling worm. With ordinary care an artificial bait lasted for a long period.

In the last few years I have asked many fly casters the reason that they had become such persistent, ardent followers of bait casting. Very few of them paused before making their reply; the explanation which came from most of them consisted in these statements: They could take bass especially by bait casting when they could not with a fly-rod outfit, and fish streams and lakes where bass seldom rose to flies, and, in the end, bass which took artificial lures of the large sort everywhere ran larger in size than those fooled with fly-fishing artifices, and they derived as much pleasure in learning accuracy by casting at the spots where bass lurked as they did at shooting at a target with a rifle. Further, they were prepared for every exigency of bass fishing, whether they were in deep water, or shallow; the sight of a bass smashing at a lure of any sort was something worth coming miles to witness.

Whatever criticism might at one time have been encouraged by the sport of bait casting becoming so popular and numbering thousands of anglers in its folds, lost all its possible merit when bait casters developed rods as light as any fly rods, and lighter lines for taking large fish than the most ethical fly casters had ever conceived possible.

With the progress of bait casting the sport got its real, permanent momentum from the people who engaged in the manufacture of fishing tackle. They were extremely modern and fully visioned the possibilities of the sport. Immediately they displayed their confidence through that master announcer of everything which becomes of service to the big sporting public, National Advertising. They exploited bait casting and bait-casting products in all the outdoor magazines to such a vast extent that they sold the sport of bait casting to hundreds of thousands of anglers almost before they marketed their products. The competition which developed among manufacturers increased the exploitation to such a degree that it can be well said that advertising in a short while made more actual anglers than fly casting which had been in vogue for such a long period.

CHAPTER II

BAIT-CASTING RODS

WHEN a sport of any kind goes through the transition which bait casting has in recent years we find that the old tools used go quickly into discard; and, however much the warring of traditions carries on some in the hands of what are known as practically old-timers, modern practical ideas inevitably are incorporated in the rods most used by the great army who go annually to lakes and streams for the purpose of flinging an artificial lure to attract some variety of game fish. Thus we are easily able to see the reason that one type of rod has superseded another, though many of us took a long, long time before we became apprised of their real merit.

Bait casters of years back thought that they had arrived at a perfect type when they regarded as perfection rods of eight, and eight and a half feet with the reel seat above the hand. This was nothing more than a stiff live-bait rod, or else a fly rod of extra stiff action with the reel seat changed to accommodate the sport of bait casting. The length and action were not the best, yet we were loath to admit it. Such a rod at present would be estimated only as exceedingly unwieldy and detracting considerably from the art of getting a lure out any distance from the angler. Furthermore, the accuracy which has now been attained could not with such a rod even be approximated. Still the old rods are held in veneration by many, and their owners cannot accept any alteration in model without regarding it as a direct flouting of both their sport and the means by which they enjoy it.

The length of bait-casting rods has gone through several stages, and, like everything else, the happy medium ultimately obtained. Not long ago thousands suddenly became enamored of rods of extreme shortness. They had appeal. They could be carried easily in a suitcase, and casting could be fairly well practiced in the brush, and they were used so consistently that great numbers of anglers began to consider anything longer than four feet as a rod of excessive length, though many were reconciled to the addition of an extra six inches. Some went so far as to prefer three-foot rods. But all these short rods were a quick development in the sport due to the obvious presence of heavy lures, whether of the artificial minnow type, or spoons weighted with a generous sinker. Yet with such rods accuracy was uncertain. It was all right if you could hit near your object with them, and such things as using the wrist alone and the value of a springy action were hardly given credit for existence in the minds of anglers. Naturally modes of casting were not of the highest order. When a fisherman could cast his lure with a side-arm movement, depending upon the weight of the lure to carry it out entirely, he was well enough pleased with his art. He caught fish, so what more had he need to worry about?

Short rods were thought to be the most convenient in boats, for as long as only the old side-arm movement was used, a longer rod would not only endanger another occupant of the boat, but also it would have the bad habit of striking the lure on its side. Shortness was estimated at a premium, and continued to be regarded so for a long time; in fact, particularly in the South, the vogue of the extremely short rod has not yet been curtailed to any great degree among certain classes.

15

Practice makes perfect, and the perfection attained by certain casters immediately brought about a new era in bait-casting rods. Not only was this the cause of the change in types of rods, but ethical anglers decided that it was not difficult to bring up the sport of bait casting to the same degree of excellence in every way as fly casting. In other words, by using light tackle, they aimed at giving a fighting game fish the same chances for escape as did the fly fisherman. Angling history at present proves that they accomplished it, though it was mighty hard to convince many obdurate fly casters that bait casting was anything more than flinging out in the water a wooden image of something upon which fish feed. Naturally the fish struck at it, and were reeled in as unceremoniously as a man drawing a bucket of water out of the well. It was strange to listen to the old fly casters tell how much bait casters lacked sportsmanship, and how they ignored the right of bass or other game fish not to be taken without giving them every opportunity to display their vigorous, gamy militancy.

Came eventually tournament casting, and, with it, visions of what ought to be accorded fighting fish. More actual tests with rods occurred than at

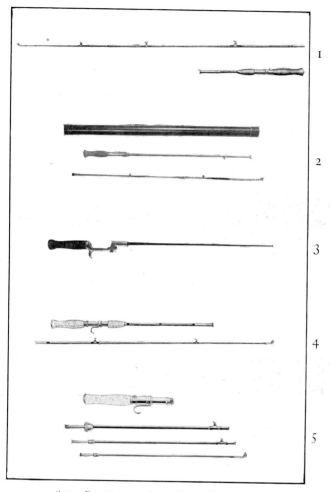

SPLIT BAMBOO AND STEEL BAIT CASTING RODS

1. Bamboo bait casting rod for half-ounce lures
2. Bamboo bait casting rod for quarter-ounce lures
3. Solid steel bait casting rod
4. Bamboo bait casting rod for five-eighths-ounce lures
5. Locking joint, steel bait casting rod

any previous period. Right away a type of rod developed which was singularly whippy and helped an angler amazingly to cast light lures, lures as small as one-quarter ounce. A model was made almost standard, and designs arrived commensurate with the expediency of larger baits and large fish. The tests given them proved that they were the best types, and accordingly American manufacturers commenced to build rods for real anglers' specifications instead of ones that approximated bait-casting ideas solely.

Bait casting owes much of its popularity to the steel rod. Its presence was noted not long after the sport came into an active state of existence.

I do not think I am playing with the elasticity of my imagination when I state that more tests concerning lengths and types were made with these in the early days of the sport than with any other kind. Furthermore, the variety in lengths and designs brought about every conceivable idea on the subject for permanent maintenance of types. They were sold at various prices, from a few dollars up, but never at very high ones. Thus a country boy for a small sum could equip himself and get a lot out of the sport which somehow

17

the exigencies of fly fishing had invariably denied him.

I have to bow to the steel rod, though for the highest type of bait casting it is not regarded as the tool *par excellence*. But it was the very thing that called for the first gamut in lengths, and a satisfactory solution. It accommodated itself to many phases, most of them still existing in the form of rods of many pieces to go in a short space, extremely short rods for both casting and trolling, telescope fishing rods, and some excellent locking devices wherein were incorporated efficient means to prevent tantalizing slipping of sections, or twisting, while casting was being done.

As things stand to-day, steel rods are used all over the bait-casting world, with cheap or expensive guides, at all prices and lengths, and combining almost every improvement known to modern artistry on the subject. While we will not attempt to reconcile a bait caster of the tournament class or light lure class to them, it suffices to say that, practically, the steel rod is a rod for the masses and will stand a great deal of rough treatment, last a long time, and help much in the bait-casting pastime. The best steel bait-casting rods are made of heavy gauge crucible steel, finished in high-class baked enamel, and equipped like those of the finest bamboo manufacture.

During the last few years an unexpected new type of steel rod appeared. Instead of being hollow and tubular in type as the recognized standard steel rod, it is made of solid steel just like a fencing foil, with the proper tempering by a secret process to incorporate in it the casting resiliency and power of a split bamboo rod, which in nearly every way its action comes close to resembling. Instead of being made of several sections like the first steel rods, the rod and handle alone make the complete outfit, the handle detachable, with a case provided for carrying them conveniently. It is a practical one-piece rod, made on lines found in the regular standard types.

While the steel rods had much to do with bringing about ideas on the subject of the right lengths for bait casting, those of split bamboo ultimately solved the problem as near as it ever will be, considering that personal predilections have most to do with the subject. Strange to say, tournament casting causes more experimenting for distance and accuracy than any other branch of the sport. Thus it happened that a rod five or five and a half feet in length was found most serviceable for all-around fishing, and the one for bait casting on the tournament casting platform, according to individual preferences, ran the list of from five and a half feet, six feet, six feet three and even with some attained the length of six and a half feet.

The part split bamboo played in fly fishing occurred similarly in bait casting. As soon as this material was made up in bait-casting rods it spelled the doom of all other rods of wooden material, though, before it was thoroughly tested in the pastime, lancewood, Bethabara, and even hickory shared popularity.

But soon bait casters discovered that the necessary qualities that were in bamboo were partly deficient in the wooden affairs. They cast well, but were slow and none of them failed to suffer from an ugly set after they were fished with any length of time. Their serviceability probably would have been better recognized had anglers known then how to care for them and only used certain ones for specific lures.

In the chapter on fly rods we have gone into the matter of the manufacture of split bamboo fly rods pretty deeply. As it does not differ

20

from the making of bait-casting rods we will not dwell further on the subject here.

In selecting bait-casting rods it is a good plan to take a few rods in your hand, assemble them, and then decide which length you will like best. Short rods of four feet will be too stiff for bait casting under most conditions; the five- or five-and-a-half foot lengths are specially recommended. Choose whatever weight you prefer but remember that action counts most. There must be a sort of springy action to all bait-casting rods; it is required for propelling the lure any distance. Therefore, though we need a springy, fairly light rod for the standard five-eighths ounce lures, this must be increased in lightness and whippiness when we think of using one-fourth and one-half ounce lures. If we use the rod particularly suitable for the five-eighths-ounce lures, we will have some difficulty in casting the lighter ones effectively. Then, remember, too, that when we get hold of a typical light lure rod we fall so in love with its action that we cannot resist the tendency to cast the larger lures with it. While it will doubtless achieve the object, before long the lightweight will suffer from the weight imposition and show a bad bow almost before you conceive such an affliction possible. The regular lures for musky casting are noticeably heavy, and require a stiff rod not only for getting them out properly but also for fighting those big tigerish fellows that exceed bass in poundage by quite a large margin.

Every angler falls in love with a light whippy bait-casting rod. The feeling of it takes absolute possession; nevertheless, there are things which must not be overlooked during the thrill experienced while they are in our hands. There are numerous fishing contingencies; every rod must have the power to turn a fighting fish from brush, weeds and rocks, as well as logs and submerged trees, glaring possibilities in every stream or lake where the fighting denizens invariably try to effect their release from the inhibitive bit of steel. Many rods are too light to rough fish in the least when it is most necessary; they ought to be avoided to some extent unless the water is free from such customary angling impediments.

We have never favored what is known as an all-purpose bait-casting rod—one for every sort of game fish. Reverse the handle, and lo! you have something which has been termed a fly rod. Facts militate against one rod of a quality for a special purpose combining all the requisites for others.

22

The last and the most sensible pronouncement on the subject is the way many skilled bait casters carry their all-purpose possessions in compact form. They have a separate handle which fits all rods they bring along; that is, they have the end of the butt joint of all their rods of different action encased in a male ferrule which fits snugly in one handle. In this manner they are equipped for all sorts of game fish, and the different waters in which they are found.

For a long time rod makers never made much progress toward providing other than a regular reel seat. In the bait-casting rod obviously it was above the handle, but constantly, after casting for a short while, owing to the pressure exerted upon it, the reel began to slip off as it worked its way from the circling bands. The first thing used to avoid this was the finger hook which held the reel in place by means of the angler holding to it while casting. After a time many locking devices appeared, and the simpler ones found a hearty welcome from anglers because they prevented reels slipping and locked so well that the annoyance of slipping no longer existed. See that such is on your casting rod; it will keep the temper in an amiable state and thus assist much in fishing.

The finger hooks really are effective, though of ancient origin, we are forced to admit, but in packing in small cases they are in the way, taking almost as much room as would otherwise serve to accommodate an extra light rod.

Rod shorteners, extra tips for casting or trolling, and similar devices are worth carrying along on a fishing trip, as they are mighty handy when trouble comes from breaking and in other ways, but so far they are mostly within the province of steel rods.

A variety of guides is manufactured for casting rods, and almost all serve their purpose effectively. It is pretty hard to account for tastes, though agate and imitation agate guides are the most seen on modern rods; one fellow likes them exceedingly large and another as small as possible, and the tip tops, or angle-casting tops, have countless followers of stirrup patterns or more abbreviated ones. Nevertheless, they all do the work, except that the very large ones are considerably in the way, though they permit the out-running line to travel smoothly. As for materials, we have mentioned the most lauded agate, or the very effective glass imitation, gamix; and the present-day serviceable competitor of agate, tungsten, must not be disregarded.

Some anglers and tournament casters show a marked partiality for one-piece bait-casting rods. Obviously they have amazing qualities of action to warrant their praise. But their greatest drawback is the room they take when traveling and this cannot be well overcome if the one-piece idea and its charming action is to be carried out. They are used without traveling inconvenience in waters not remote, or on the fast approaching popular tournament platform.

I am exceedingly partial to leather carrying cases for bait-casting rods, particularly when a number of rods are to be taken on a long trip. They are wonderful protectors of their valuable contents, though those of cheaper material, having properties considerably like leather, are not to be despised. For the regular casting rods aluminum cases are furnished, made chiefly for single rods. Their lightness and the protection which they afford are worthy of notice, but never forget to place in the ends paper or cotton to prevent the agates in the casting tops, or the solid tungsten casting tops, from being broken inadvertently when the container strikes some hard substance.

CHAPTER III

BAIT-CASTING LINES AND CASTING
GUIDES

WHEN bait casting came into such universal vogue, and the possibilities of great skill seemed likely, anglers and manufacturers began to put their heads together to learn what was the best all-round material for every variety of casting. After exhaustive tests, silk proved the most serviceable when it was braided properly over a core, and when the dimensions were the same from one end of the casting line to the other.

Silk is smooth, has easy running qualities, and, for its fineness, is possessed of superior strength, though it loses a small part of its strength after it becomes wet. It can be used satisfactorily only in fresh-water angling. Deterioration attacks it quickly after contact with salt water. But no line is so easy to thumb as one of silk, and, however much experiments have been made with cotton and linen, no entirely satisfactory bait-casting lines have ever been produced from these materials.

None of them keeps so near the same size when soaked up in water as silk.

The average bait caster for bass, large trout, wall-eyed and northern pike and pickerel prefers lines from nine-pound test to twenty-five pound test in strength, though there is never any need, for these fish, of any line heavier than a twelve-pound test, or even nine-pound test, if handled with care. I know of one angler in the Rainy River country who never uses a line even for the largest muskies of over nine-pound test. The writer never uses any heavier, and one time fought a wicked battling rainbow trout in the lower Nipigon River—one of the few that occasionally run up this river—which weighed fourteen and one-half pounds. This was in extremely fast water, and the fish was given every opportunity to break the line, but with the whippy casting rod he never succeeded in doing it.

Sometimes men fish with lighter lines than this; it simmers down, however, rather to stunt work than practical fishing.

Here is one difference in casting lines: heavy lines are neither so easy to cast with nor to thumb. The fine nine-pound test lines are quite strong

27

enough, but they wear out quickly after a few days of steady fishing. Further, expert anglers arrange their line requisites for personal casting comfort by using a heavy line for large and weighty lures and quite the reverse for the light ones.

In recent years, a very serviceable line known as waterproof silk line has come on the market. It is guaranteed for a long period against rotting and the other arch enemy of silk lines, mildew. Some lines have one fault, which is hardness and stiffness. This wears away with a few days of constant fishing.

While a lot of argument has been indulged in over the respective merits of hard-braided and soft-braided silk lines, the demarcation between the two rests in the fact that soft-braided lines are the easier to cast but they wear out very quickly. Hard-braided lines are very strong and last often an entire season, but they are by no means so easy to thumb as the other kind. However, there is, on account of their lasting qualities, a noticeable trend toward waterproofed hard-braided lines, even in the small sizes. The manufacturers are making rapid strides in these lines by finishing them so that even when first used they are as easy to thumb as what is known as the soft variety.

To get good results from lines, they must have careful attention. Frequently, a greasy reel will cause quick deterioration in a line. Oil will get on the thumb and fingers and quickly impart itself to the line, which may be injured by the effect of the grease.

Another cause of lines breaking is the defective line guide. In cheap rods, guides of none too hard metal are used; first, the silk lines sever these guides, then the cuts sever the line. Imitation or genuine agates without being noticed become cracked and consequently cut lines, when, in most instances, the angler blames the poor quality of the line instead of his lack of watchfulness. I have seen anglers time and again rebuke dealers for selling a certain brand of silk casting line. They declared that such a line broke at the slightest strain; when the cause was not inferiority of the material but a cracked guide which the complainant had never taken pains to discover. If you use too fine lines with heavy lures, they wear very rapidly the first few feet on account of the rubbing in the tip top.

An angler should watch his line continually.

Every three hours or so he should break off several feet of the end where the most wear takes place. Neglect of this precaution results in the loss of many fish at the moment of landing them.

Every day lines should be dried in the shade or at intervals between fishing. Naturally, they dry more quickly in the sun, but little is gained because the sun causes the line to become very brittle. A line dries gradually in the shade. But always remember when we advise drying a line, we mean thoroughly drying it. The outside may look dry, but, if the line has not been submitted long enough to exposure the core may still be damp. There are several special line-drying spools which can be dissembled and packed in a small space for convenient carrying on a fishing trip. But no one will ever be at loss at home for a place upon which to dry a line. Wind it from bedpost to bedpost, or on a chair, and leave it until morning. Never put it away in your tackle kit, or anywhere else, while it is still wet or damp, if you value your line in the least.

Bait casters for many salt-water species of game fish, on account of the immediate deterioration of the silk line on contact with their habitat, now use a new type of linen line. It is fine, strong, but yet a little too hard for comfortable casting.

The first guides used on bait-casting rods were what was known as the trumpet variety. Until the sport developed in popularity those who started it never realized what a guide would have to undergo from the use of silk lines. Further, trumpet guides in their construction left much to be desired, as they retarded some the free running of the lines. They were made of supposedly hard materials, but even the tip guide, where most strain and wear occur constantly, was not sufficiently hard to prevent cutting of the line. Later they were manufactured of such hard material as file-proof steel. But the best were yet too soft, and finally manufacturers hit upon the idea of using genuine agates or garnix, a glass imitation of agate, and tungsten.

Garnix is only a superior hard glass colored to resemble agate. It gives just as good service as agate and possibly better than badly worked agates. As you cannot always trust the human element, often a negligent workman causes a rough agate to appear on a rod, and thus a fine line wears faster than it should. An agate is hard to surpass, as the vital part of the necessary guides needed in a casting rod. It will stand quite a lot of abuse if mounted properly. Its only competitor is the modern material, tungsten.

Tungsten guides have become quite popular and are seen on many fine rods. They are not beautiful, but they are exceedingly light and absolutely will not cut from the continual use of a silk line. They are brittle and will crack like agate, if they come violently in contact with a hard object. But they have an outstanding advantage in this respect which many anglers ignore. When they break, a fairly big part is severed; at least, sufficiently big for an angler to notice immediately; and thus be able to tie on another in its place. Agates often crack but do not chip off, so that the injury is not observed until a valuable line is ruined.

One never realizes the worth of a rod case unless on a long journey. On account of their prominent mountings of agate and tungsten, casting rods are more susceptible to injury than fly rods. A jar of any sort may break a guide. Hence it is well to remember what was said at the end of Chapter II about the importance of using a case that will afford sure protection to the rods, mountings, and guides.

CHAPTER IV

SERVICEABLE CASTING REELS

IN early days we were often inclined to marvel at the respect that old-time bait casters lavished upon reels which had been in their possession for a great number of years, at the loving expressions, the rapt admiration with which they regarded each and every part of their structure. They spun them around with a twirl of the venerated handle, and, listening to the hum, placed them close to their ears in order to try to detect any flaw in action, such as despised lateral movement. But it was the way anglers had of showing their treasures to their friends; of exhibiting their wonderful qualities. And they are no different from anglers of to-day who possess these old, high-grade reels. They are as devout in their worship of them and hold them in highest esteem. Whence one sees that a good reel is the key to the sport of bait casting. The quality of material and workmanship which anglers appreciated in the early moments are just as valuable now as they were then.

The records of early-day bait casting seem indelibly associated with the names of such makers as Meek, Milam and Talbot, and even now the luster on them remains untarnished since they are still as popular as they ever were and are yet regarded as particular standards of a certain high-class type. This number, however, has been augmented with the coming of South Bend, Heddon, Shakespeare, Pfleuger, Meisselbach, Foss and a host of others of lesser note, who have incorporated the necessary principles of the above-named trail blazers and the addition of certain mechanical arrangements which help to simplify the art of bait casting.

The simplicity of the old reels has never been improved upon. The principles arrived at in their construction were just what anglers required for bait casting: smooth running and retrieving, owing to the efficiency of the spiral, no lateral movement of the spool, and the bearings enclosed so that they are almost dust proof yet easily uncovered for the purpose of oiling. The value of a reel for casting is represented in all these items. With care, the wear of constant work will have no injurious effects upon them, though they are called upon to accomplish tasks under various adverse conditions which, doubtless, would wreck many instruments of more formidable appearing structure.

Often, when asked which reel a bait caster ought to buy, we are inclined to hesitate, but invariably we fall back on the reply: The best that money can purchase. Then, we are prone to add, with the certitude of experience, that in this way we are doing much to add to the pleasures of the sport and ultimately save considerable money for the angler. The arguments in favor of buying the highest class reels are simple and convincing. With care, they will last the lifetime of yourself and your son. They facilitate casting, give additional pleasure, and are money-savers, because no reels made of cheap materials on a big production basis which sell for a small sum are of any service after a few weeks' or a month's use. The exception to this rule is seldom seen.

If you are willing to purchase a high-priced reel, give it care. Clean its exterior every time you use it, and oil the bearings. Occasionally, take it apart and clean it with gasoline by placing it in a tumbler of this fluid and wiping dry the parts with a piece of tissue paper. Do not touch it with a cloth. Before assembling it, place on the gears with a toothpick a tiny amount of vaseline.

Many anglers like jeweled bearings, but they have little advantage in fishing over such material as perfect phosphor bronze or kindred hard metals, and are more likely to break if dropped on, or knocked against some hard substance.

Cheap reels are mostly made for beginners and those who have no idea of the gruelling work which a bait-casting reel has to undergo. In order to make profit on them, they are made on a big production basis of cheap material and, on account of the expense attached to it, they can never be subjected to severe tests for fitting and similar matters by trained hands. Most of them are substitutes for an actual reel and are expected to carry over the possessor until he cares to buy the quality kind that his sport exacts.

While the English have striven to produce a perfect fly-casting reel, so far their activities have never been devoted to bait-casting models. The latter-day inventions to help anglers are antibacklash and level-winding devices. The advantages of antibacklash reels to a beginner, or an experienced fisherman who has never been able to mas-

MULTIPLYING AND SINGLE ACTION REELS

ter the art of bait casting, are incalculable. Mechanically, an antibacklash reel performs the function of the human thumb, which is to keep an ever-so-light drag on the spool to prevent what is known as backlashing; to wit, the reel running faster than the lure causes the line to run round itself if a drag of some kind is not used. Thousands and thousands start in fishing with these antibacklash reels and have good success from the very first hour they try. They are not expensive, and the material and workmanship are good.

Another device on modern reels which aids bait casters considerably is that of the level winder. It also takes the place of the human finger to distribute the line evenly over the spool. It necessitates, otherwise, some expertness to do this properly. If it is not done as it should be, and more line has been spooled in one place than in another in unsightly humps, there will be the same disastrous trouble as backlashing. The level winder prevents this without any mental or physical attention on the part of the angler other than the application of a little oil daily when in use.

Probably the only argument against level-winding devices is the fact that they retard the casting action of excessively light lures, such as those weighing only one-fourth of an ounce. Those of one-half and five-eighths of an ounce can be accurately cast with them. Many anglers who confine their fishing sport entirely to trolling invariably are in possession of reels with level-winding devices. There is then no danger of trouble from the line accumulating all on one place on the spool through hasty and inconsiderate reeling caused by the excitement of fighting a fish.

Big sellers among reels of this character are those which are equipped both with the antibacklash and level-winding devices.

A good feature in these latter-day reels is not only their sturdiness, but also the fact that, if a part is broken or they get otherwise out of order, they can be taken apart and the defective piece replaced, for the manufacturers provide the repair parts for anglers to carry with them.

We have one type of reel which is of single action but which has never yet been regarded in the same esteem as the standard bait-casting reel with quadruple action. Their great fault is that they are too bulky. The line is not so easily guided. They are of very large size because it is the size of the windlass which supplants the

38

quadruple action obtained by the gear contrivances in the old dependables.

It was not so many years ago that a myriad of bait-casting inventions appeared on the market to hasten the act of retrieving the line. There were reels of five- and seven-multiple type; that is, they wound the spool five or seven times with one revolution of the handle. They certainly did expedite retrieving the lure, but they were rank failures when it came to fighting a big fish.

One model was built with a sort of ratchet handle. It was worked like a pump gun fore end. It was difficult to cast a five-eighths of an ounce lure with them accurately and they had the bad habit of failing to function during the retrieve when most needed. Some lasted only as long after they were tried out as the advertising appropriation of their makers.

Quite a bit of *éclat* has come to certain manufacturers from their efforts at putting on the market high-grade reels and ones of moderate price with what are known as free spools. In order to facilitate casting the instant the lure is flung, the gear is disengaged and the outgoing lure travels from a spool which is unhampered in any manner. As soon as the angler starts retrieving the lure, the gears are once more engaged and perform their task well. With some of the very high-class tournament reels the caster performs the act of engaging and disengaging the actuating gears, while the free spool reels made purposely for fishing perform the act mechanically.

We cannot stress too much your giving your reel almost as much attention as your watch, if not more. This care will repay you well. Every one should have a solid leather case to protect his reel against possible bumps to and from the fishing grounds, and against injury from dirt and dust entering the precious mechanism.

As bait casting is done at such a distance from the haunts of the fish, we need never worry about the brightness of the reel. The metal most in use is German silver or one of similar alloys, while the cheap ones are merely stamped thin sheet iron, known to the trade as tin plate, and nickeled.

CHAPTER V

THE ART OF BAIT CASTING

PERHAPS the greatest assets in bait casting are poise and self-confidence, but before either is developed certain essentials have to be mastered. While writing these lines, we are forced to visualize two classes who wish to learn properly the modern art of flinging an artificial lure with a whippy, abbreviated rod—we use the word "abbreviated" to point out the distinct difference in length between the short bait-casting rod and the universally long rod with which fly fishing is performed. There are two types of pupils to think about; one of them has never had any previous experience in bait casting; the other has been fishing in this manner for years, but, having started in bad form, has kept it up almost perversely, one might say. Of the two, obviously the latter is the more difficult to set right. Sentimentally, he thinks his bad form is correct until he sees an expert casting; then he is usually too sensitive about corrections to have them register as speedily as they should.

Women, like other beginners, who wish to learn, particularly when they have made no previous attempts, absorb the fundamentals quickly and become experts as fast as men. Once they feel the thrill of a fish at the end of their line, thereafter they are converts to bait casting. Some of the most graceful, efficient casters I ever saw were women. Everything in their being responds quickly to the springy, short rod, the hum of the reel and the desire to strike accurately the objective at which they aim. One thing most noticeable in the performance of women bait casters is their fairness to their quarry, as they seem to feel more pleasure from the quality of the sport than the number of fish they take. Women are unquestionably an addition to a fishing party and they have an invariable faculty for teaching youngsters the gentle finesse of ethical angling.

The old trite saying about doing a thing right or not at all applies pertinently to bait casting. It is just as easy to learn the right methods as the obsolete and half-way ones. And this is the very reason I am stressing at the start the over-the-shoulder wrist-action style as preferable to any other sort. Naturally, I expect to find a few objections from those who have practiced side-swiping, as the side-arm style is named, because they will dwell on its utility for getting the lure under limbs of trees and other desirable places. Yet learning the straight over-the-shoulder form will increase their casting ability and ultimately they will learn to apply the wrist and forearm movement to their beloved side-swiping artistry and, in consequence, improve in smoothness and accuracy.

You will find many available places for learning and practicing. The little pond in the park or one in the outskirts of the city is ideal. If you have a lawn at home, it, too, will serve the purpose well.

Absorb these hints before beginning, then it will not be difficult to get the fundamentals into your system. First, place on your reel what is known as a filler, that is, any old casting line which is no longer of service. Do this to such an extent that it leaves sufficient room for fifty yards of casting line. Be sure that it is wound on evenly, then attach to it the silk casting line. If this is not done, you will find it harder to thumb the reel

43

on account of the extra distance the thumb has to reach. The thumb is the main instrument in the art and it must not be forgotten; it plays the part of drag and stop.

Now you are ready to begin casting after you have placed an object forty or fifty feet away from you for a target. But, first, say to yourself, over and over again, that for the present you wish only to learn accuracy—to hit the target or very close to it—and distance will take care of itself later on. At any rate, accuracy will count more than distance in fishing. While distance casting is worth mastering, it is not so important as being able to drop your lure just where you want it seventy or seventy-five feet away.

Can you momentarily picture an expert snap-shot with shotgun or rifle? He does not aim at his target and then pull, but centers his eye on the moving or stationary target and never removes it until he has pulled the trigger. I mention this because it is an important preliminary lesson in bait casting to hold your eye on your target before casting and while you are in the act of casting; it ought never to be removed until the lure has stopped its flight. Repeat this to yourself three times, and now for your first lesson in casting.

Assume an easy position facing your target. Grasp your rod firmly in your right hand, place your elbow close against your body, but relax all the wrist and forearm muscles. Now, repeat these lines to yourself and then practice all they imply before attempting to cast. Attach to your line a practice casting weight weighing five-eighths of an ounce, which is the average weight of a standard artificial lure. Reel it within five or six inches of the tip top. Be careful not to reel it hard against the tip top lest you break the latter. Point the rod toward your target, place your thumb on the spool of your reel, then quickly bring the rod up slightly over your shoulder, without moving your elbow from your body. Thus you will really control the distance back of you that it should go. Then with an easy movement, bring the rod forward and release the pressure of your thumb. Instantly your lure will start traveling. But right here you will discover a few perhaps unexpected happenings, if you have had no prior experience in casting, or have not observed others. If you release the lure too soon, it will go straight up above or behind you, and, if you release your thumb too late, the lure will suddenly drop on the ground close to you. There is always a happy

45

medium for success, and that is, in casting, to release your thumb when the rod tip is straight out on an even line with your shoulder.

For a while, though you have perfected these simple rudiments in casting, you must practice thumbing your reel. If you release your thumb entirely from the reel, it will backlash, as we told in a former chapter, because the outgoing lure imparts to the reel greater speed than that at which it is traveling, causing the loose or slack line to wind around itself in a maze of annoying tangles and snarls. Just cultivate the habit of never taking your thumb off the spool and try to realize the need of always feeling the line purring slightly against your thumb, and you will quickly become expert in casting easily and preventing backlashes.

Once more for your real start, after you have become familiar with these easily avoided intricacies in the casting game, point your rod tip at your target and center it with your eye, until your lure stops. Cast as I have advised before, with a smooth easy movement, releasing your thumb just enough from the spool for the lure to travel, but feeling it all the time with your thumb.

46

Just as your lure begins to fall within two feet of the ground, apply your thumb firmly. This will stop your lure, and keep your spool from revolving further.

If you have followed these directions, you will soon learn that the fundamentals of bait casting are simplicity itself. Soon you will learn to increase the distance you cast with no greater exertion, but if you commence with a jerky motion or try to throw hard, immediately your thumb will be pulled off the spool and a nasty backlashing of the line will ensue.

After your lure alights near or on your target, it is up to you to retrieve it. So be prepared to remember another thing, which is as important as thumbing your spool, and that is to wind your line level. Transfer your rod to your left hand and with a back and forward movement of your forefinger and thumb distribute your line evenly on your spool. If you wind the line unevenly, you will be unable to thumb it and, consequently, another backlash will occur.

As you become gradually versed in the art, you will transfer the rod to your left hand as the lure is within the last few feet of its flight, achieving it almost mechanically without any mental impression that you are doing it. Most expert anglers transfer the rod to the left hand while the lure is in flight. But it is well at first not to attempt it until the lure has finished traveling its ultimate distance.

Dry-line casting is a mere improvement of the style mentioned above. The line is kept dry when fishing all the time, except a few feet near the lure. A dry line runs more easily than a wet one, hence it encourages exceedingly deft casting. To accomplish this, the rod is transferred to the left hand when the lure is nearly at the end of its flight, but, instead of having the tip point toward the object, it is held in a vertical position, and the reeling is done while the rod is pointed that way. This keeps the line out of the water, and if any perfection has been attained, assures a dry line all day. In fishing, it is done mostly with light surface or semi-surface casting baits. With heavy lures, the dry line will cut the thumb, even though it is protected with adhesive tape, and most anglers object very much to casting with thumb stalls.

Many hold their reels down when casting, with the handle toward the sky. Many seem to get a better wrist movement when in this position. But the majority prefer casting with the reel in a horizontal position.

We are not inclined to deride side casting, as some do. It is quite necessary in the larger part of the South, where trees so closely overhang the water. But the wrist movement can be applied nicely by the side-swiper, and both relieves his art of extra labor and improves his accuracy. Naturally, irresponsible side-swipers brought hatred for their method by the number of times, in a boat, they threatened the other occupants with the danger of a lure's striking them—something which has more than once occurred.

The art of bait casting brings to mind the advisability of ethical deportment while two are casting from the same boat. Never cast across another man's line; never cause any disturbance which might frighten the fish. Always offer him the front of the boat, and the next time he will do the same for you. Never stand up in a boat.

The price of skilled casting is constant practice. Practice whenever you have the opportunity and perfect the prominent feature in which most are weak, thumbing the reel. In time your art will become so deft that you will be able to hit close to almost anything you wish, and you will learn, by manipulation of the thumb and wrist, to drop the lure silently in the lurking places of bass, when they are in a mood to take fright at the slightest disturbance.

CHAPTER VI

CASTING FLIES AND PORK STRIPS

THE average bait caster has far more knowledge of flies for his sport than most anglers will give him credit for. His category is both large and amazingly varied. A lot of the old-timers who have followed this method of taking fish for years are as exacting about the kind they use for different waters, seasons of the year and weather conditions as the most enthusiastic purist who wields a light rod for trout of all varieties. You may argue with them about colors, sizes, and everything associated with flies, but when you have exhausted all your verbal ammunition you will find them just as perverse as the most ethical trout fishermen. I have seen some fly books owned by casters of artificial baits which for quantity and variety would make even a salmon fisherman green with envy. And in most cases one book was not sufficient for their repertoire; they had to have two and three. The colorations were so extensive they baffled any sort of problematical enumeration.

Let us take a list of the bucktails and then we begin just to get into what seems to have the lead in the fly line of bait casters. The hair on deer tails ever since first used has retained an immense following. The singular insectlike crawl it has when moved the least in water is regarded as the main source of its potency. It is tied on all shapes and bends of hooks, but universally, like all bait-casting flies, on straight-eyed hooks. They are the only ones which will not turn over awkwardly and interfere with the action of the spoon or lure to which they are attached; for all casting flies have in advance of them some sort of attachment which creates the necessary flash to attract game fish. In fact, my own experience in bait casting, especially watching others, records that I have seen bait casters for trout only who used occasionally flies with no such auxiliary to aid them, only weight to serve the angler as an aid to fling them out.

Bucktail flies are exceedingly durable. Shake them after they are wet and they not only will dry out quickly, but also retain their shape and all their first potency. They come on single, double and treble hooks. Some have the body weighted with lead, and the weight thus arranged does not detract from its shapeliness. Quite a number have chenille bodies, or bodies made like standard flies. When the bodies are not weighted usually the entire spinner arrangement has an addition of a snap swivel sinker or a dipsey sinker for the needed casting weight. Some bucktail flies are strangely constructed in the form of first a short hackle, then a still shorter one, and then another. These are called minnows by the manufacturers, and there is no limit to the number of shapes and the way bucktail bodies are fashioned. Many of these flies have the hair tied in opposite directions to give them a more killing effect.

The first bucktails used were the natural colors of white, fawn, gray or brown. Some anglers consider one of these colors sufficient for all purposes and never change to others, no matter how much fishing they do. But quite a few are sincere in their devotion to colors and blends or contrasting colors, and when they have a formidable supply they feel they are well prepared to cope with any casting exigency, if they are out for bass, pike, pickerel or muskies. They feature the light colors

53

for cloudy weather or murky water and dark colors for sunny days.

Many fishermen declare contrasts of colors are what cause fish to strike best. The strictly bucktail devotee who angles a great deal is usually equipped with them. Then we see orange, salmon, blue, black, brown, red and yellow featured, and the contrast comes when the flies are tied half one color and half of another. Some may ridicule this piscatorial adherence to colors, but they do catch fish, though often we cannot explain why. One of the greatest successes I ever had fishing for small-mouth bass was with a single No. 3 spinner to which was attached a dark blue bucktail. I can swear without danger of contradiction that I never saw a live minnow that looked like it or anything connected with the food of game fish which resembled it in the least. Yet it was a producer that day from the first to the last cast I made with it.

To give additional attractiveness to bucktails one maker incorporated in his creation streamers of rooster hackle. This gave the kick of the most active pork rind strip, particularly when the separate pieces of rooster hackle that were tied in opposite directions worked back and forth, resembling exceedingly the tail movement of a live minnow. Such flies are known as streamer bucktails. This streamer effect we know well is a characteristic of many of the modern strictly fly rod lures.

The hair of fox and gray squirrel tails is a great favorite with bait casters, too. Thousands of anglers regard them in the same esteem as bucktails, and this is the reason they are tied in various forms. Their attractiveness is admitted, and no more potent black fly is ever seen on fishing waters than a fox or squirrel tail dyed black. Numbers of squirrel-tail flies are tied with streamers. But on account of the shortness of the hair the exceedingly large ganged hook styles are not covered with the hair of the woodrats. The natural hair of either the fox or gray squirrel tails is really a fish getter without the necessity of resorting to other colors and effects. The outstanding dark bar contrasts with the rest and surely ought to fill the bill for any one needing casting flies of this class.

There is a line of strictly designated hair flies, which, by the way, mostly are not made alone of hair, but the resemblance comes from the use of chicken hackles commonly found in all flies. This might be qualified by saying a good quality of stripped hackles which gives the natural hair effect. Most of the flies show opposite tyings—one way the hair is reversed and the other regular fashion, or an effective continuous combination of varied effects. All of these have an insectlike movement in water, and the colors in which they are made really show the versatility of their originators, as well as their knowledge of the things which will most bring the rise or strikes of game fish to lures of such designing. There is practically no limit to the patterns of hair flies—no more than to the kind of feathers from which they are made, or of which they are a part or a combination. Very seldom, however, are they seen made with weighted bodies. A body of lead prevents the tying artistry necessary to their body conformation and beauty.

Before going deeper in the matter of casting flies it is noteworthy that the cork-bodied bass bugs and feather minnows are of late years frequently found used in connection with spinners by expert and ordinary casters. Some are so enthusiastic about them that they attach them to the regular pork rind spinners instead of the pork strip itself. Of course only those with the straight eye-ringed hooks will serve best. The advocates of these valuable lures claim justly that the head of the bugs and minnows brings about an extra enticing kick when the bait is reeled quickly or slowly.

No class of bait casters can be found who have not in their tackle kits feathered flies for attaching to spinners. They are manufactured in the standard patterns, and many other creations as well. There are a lot made with the regular bodies of chenille, tinsel and silk. The weighted bodies have great popularity with anglers. They save the addition of a sinker of any sort, and the body shape can be perfectly carried out; also, when the bodies are decorated with the modern enamels, they can hardly be told from a wrapped body, and such flies have not the habit of jumping back and catching on the line when the cast is being effected or when the lure is being reeled in cross current. Many of them are almost perfectly weedless. Tied with reverse wings of large size the hook is sufficiently protected to keep it from fouling on snags, weeds and rocks. Further, by the arrangement of one or two feathers, or the addition of this number, a lure is made to ride the water properly, and thus avoid twisting in whatever manner they are fished.

The bait caster who is most devoted to the use of all sorts of feathered, bucktail, and various hair flies has the advantage of being able to go almost anywhere with a very light equipment, and yet be able to bring the strikes of all sorts of game fish very regularly. With a fly book containing the different combinations and a number of spinners and casting weights and swivels he has an outfit in compact form for use almost anywhere bass, pike, pickerel, wall-eyes and muskies are found.

Something about flies or pork rind is included in this chapter because, like the majority of bait-casting flies, they are separate attachments to certain special lures. They are also used as additional attractions on many flies and casting spoons. Quite in conformity with the progress of other tackle requisites, very seldom do we see an angler carrying along his pork and cutting it V-shape to wriggle enticingly behind a lure as formerly. It was a greasy mess at best and did not endure long. Even the slender pork chunk is relegated to antiquity and the affair of commerce, stored in un-leakable, capped bottles, takes its place, just as

58

the pork strip is prepared, for the convenience of anglers, in liquids which insure against discoloration or loss of valuable color.

The pork strip of commerce has come to stay. All the grease is kept away from rods, the hands and tackle kits, and it comes ready cut in all sizes and shapes better than the majority of anglers can ever hope to shape it. Manufacturers make different types. The favorite seems to be shaped so that it has a side-to-side movement and tail kick like a swimming minnow. When one of these is hooked to a casting fly, it gives the appearance of a very bold minnow trying to seize the fly, something no game fish will permit to take place in its presence without endeavoring to grab both at one gulp. Pieces of pork are also cut out to resemble frogs and minnows. They are universally recommended by anglers as infallible, though everything else fails.

CHAPTER VII

THE VERSATILE WOODEN LURES

ANGLERS hold two different opinions of the wooden lures used in bait casting, and, while we are regarding them either from a sentimental or practical viewpoint, it is not out of place to say that irrespective of their conformation or construction such lures are all best known to the public as plugs. Even the erstwhile designated underwater minnow is universally classed as a plug, as well as anything made of wood for angling purposes constructed either to resemble a minnow or a contraption of the same material of indefinite coloration which creates a splash in the water.

The opinion of one class of overethical anglers is that a plug, on account of its supply of one, three or five treble hooks, is a barbarous invention which ought to have no place in an angler's tackle kit. On the other hand, the opponents argue very correctly that the use of treble hooks on a plug ought not to be condemned because a game fish, during its leaps or flounces, can cast out of

60

its mouth a treble hook far more easily than a single.

Doing the best to avoid redundancy in trying to settle an argument which will never be settled to the satisfaction of everybody, we can state with no chance of refutation that on account of the size of plugs more hooks are required to hang a fish than on any other lure. Between trebles and single hooks, if we view all angles of sportsmanship with unprejudiced eyes, actual tests will show that it is much easier for a fish to free itself from a treble hook than from a single. Personal experiences mean nothing to the average angler so that I will merely add that the real solution of this is the fact that a treble hook can penetrate only so far as the bend of the shank, so that the closeness of its mates welded together at the shank prevents its going any farther, though the angler may exert all his skill and strength. On the other hand, a single hook is obviously more deadly than a treble on account of its faculty for penetrating; and chances for escape are eliminated a great deal. Furthermore, it can be constructed in many bends and shapes which are not possible with the others.

In addition to the above, we are prone to think

that anglers buy what they want. Modern plugs can be equipped with single hooks as desired, but the call is exceedingly limited for this sort, though one of the largest manufacturers in the world furnishes single detachable hooks for plugs. They have wonderful holding qualities and, on account of the hooks being detachable, can be carried loose in a coat pocket without danger, as formerly, of catching on to everything they touch.

The first wooden plug used by anglers palpably was of the present-day underwater type. It resembled a minnow and gradually it had attached to the front, the rear, or both, small bright metal spinners to create the necessary splash in order to attract fish. The success of the anglers brought merited prominence almost at the very moment the plugs began to appear on the market; and they stood high in favor until another type appeared, closely resembling it but having for its qualities the real action of a swimming, darting or crippled minnow. This lure was called a plug. It was painted in various colorations, but the thing which created its singular movement when being reeled in the water was a particular grooved or slanting shaped head, which, on encountering water resistance, caused it to travel beneath the surface and disport itself with amazing antics. It not only became popular immediately on account of its great fish-catching qualities, but it had tremendous additional value in the eyes of both experienced and inexpert anglers because it floated. It was a money saver. With all the old types of underwater lures, if a backlash was encountered while the lure was moving in the water, the lure sank and consequently very often was lost by the hooks hanging to a rock, log or root. On the contrary, with the new plug devoid of spinners, as soon as anything on the part of the angler caused it to stop, immediately it came to the surface of lake or stream and floated all the while it was at rest, giving the manipulator of the reel ample time to unravel the entanglement without losing his precious artificial lure. Furthermore, if an angler happened to cast such a wooden deceit and found that in its route it was about to encounter a log, he could stop reeling just when near it and permit the bait to float slowly over it or jump the obstacle by a slight motion of the rod.

To-day the most popular artificial lure is the cigar-shaped one of wood with a grooved head. Others with straight slanting head or metal plates run a close second. Some of them combine both surface and underwater properties in one lure. This is done either by shifting the metal plate or changing the place to which the casting line is attached, thus offering an opportunity to an angler with a single lure to go after game fish as deep or as close to the surface as he wishes.

When artificial lures became popular the numerous ways in which they were decorated were past enumerating. Manufacturers had assortments. For a long time they vied with each other in bringing out a new coloration or a promiscuity of colorations. Their elaborations defied classification, if not accurate description. From the first, this tremendous group included everything from likenesses of natural minnows to gold and silver tints and nuances. And still all of them had faithful followers because they actually caught fish. But the idea—the main idea—of imitating the colors of the different live minnows with which game fish are caught was never lost and the ultimate development is what is now known as scale finish, something which hundreds of years ago was an example of artistry seen on the many lacquer-finished articles made by the Japanese, and which must have invaded the minds of the numerous modern agencies who separately con-

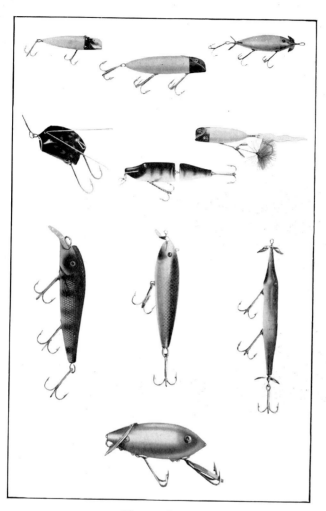

WOODEN PLUGS

ceived the various splendid scale finishes used on so many artificial baits.

The artificial lure formerly was both widely used and of many varieties. Hundreds appeared on the market. The variety of shape, too, seemed for a long time to be unlimited, but eventually they simmered down to the present supply of remarkable fishing potentialities; the cigar-shaped plug with its motive power in that amazing grooved head, the slanting plate with minnow-shaped body, and then the present minnow-shaped body, divided into sections which add to the wriggling characteristics, but yet retain their head attachments so that they travel beneath the surface at the impulse of the angler.

It is easy for any one versed in the lore of wooden lures to go deeply into the subject of colors; why and how they attract fish under different conditions. The result of it all would be practically unlimited ramifications, the narration of numerous piscatorial incidents which would convince no one that they were unalterable scientific facts.

To the amateur or the expert I have to confess that from years of experimenting with lures in most of the great inland fishing waters between the Gulf of Mexico and Hudson Bay, in the United States and Canada, I have come to the conclusion that man cannot tell in a certain stream or lake which is the best color until he tries them all and, when he thinks he has found the right one, something pops up to prove that he is still in the realm of conjecture instead of certainty; if this were not the case, the fishing sport would lose one of its chief attractions—uncertainty. When I refer to colors or color schemes featured in denoting wooden lures I feel that visibility under different circumstances counts most. I am, too, influenced by the urge to express a personal finding, and that is, strange as it may seem, on account of a lot of circumstances impossible to narrate, a color may perform well for one angler and yet achieve quite the reverse for another. I will cite a single instance to bear me out in this:

There is a particular lake which I often fish while in a mood for bait casting. Its water is influenced considerably by its only feeder, a mountain stream. In case of a freshet it becomes murky quickly, or responds to any influence of the elements in the same manner as the small river that feeds it water. One morning after a freshet I fished hard each rocky indentation, bank, or log which promised to be a likely harboring place for a bass. Not one rise did I produce. My lure was an artificial minnow of green-scale finish. Thinking that a plug with red head and white body might be better for such condition of the water, I affixed one and immediately began to take bass regularly where I had failed during the previous round of casting.

After a time of splendid fishing I met a bait caster assembling his outfit and immediately advised him that the red and white combination was the only color ensemble worth trying. But, perversely, he ignored my proffer of advice and deliberately started to use a plug which for me had been resultless—the very same scale-finish minnow which I had first cast so long. Then it was my turn to be surprised. He began to catch fish in the very places where they had refused my scale-finished offering and, before the day was over, his total surpassed mine both in size and number of fish taken.

I shall never declare that one color, or blend of colors, surpasses any other or a combination of others. This the angler must decide for himself; for the different waters and his style of fishing may effect need for variations I know nothing about. Naturally, I am willing to admit my personal preferences, listing what has performed for me best without striving to persuade others to do likewise or regarding my experiences as things to imitate. I have favorites in plugs. I brazenly confess that the colorations are: white body with red head, green- and blue-scale finish; in fact, all of the scale finishes which I regard as wonderfully potent in exceedingly or fairly clear water. Other pet predilections include gold body with red head, silver or aluminum finish with red head, rainbow chub, and spotted frog effects. With these I have faith that I can achieve everything except the conquering of my angling prejudices.

There are worlds of other color combinations which I can recommend because, in true American parlance, they deliver the goods, whether the color artistry originated from a desire to imitate the natural minnow, crawfish or tadpole. I am sure any of them which have good action will bring results if any fish in a striking mood happens to be about. The fish has to be near and in the mood. No one has ever been able with any lure to take game fish when they were not in the immediate vicinity of his cast. There is just one reference to be made on the subject of artificial

68

bait color schemes. The quality of the finish which American manufacturers put on their lures is undeniably perfect, and the result of intimate fishing experiences.

Though numbers will differ with me, my favorite color for night fishing with plugs is black. I admit that others have had remarkable success with nite-luming and other colors, but I am sentimentally loyal to what has acted well for me. There is no chance in making a mistake selecting shapes for night fishing. Only a few are designed especially for this purpose. They attract by the spluttering they make with spinners or some similiar contrivance that encounters water resistance and produces a like disturbance. Just reel them slowly and jerkily. Stop now and then, and pursue the regular manner of retrieving. I have never had much success with underwater or semi-underwater lures at night, but others have; so I shall not declare they are worthless because I could not get the finny chaps to strike them regularly.

I am firmly convinced that all anglers, tyros and experts, should experiment with each type of plug they intend to take on a fishing trip and while they are on the trip, note down mentally just what sort of antics appeal most in their waters. The necessity for offering this advice comes from the palpable fact of the differences in lures and the best ways for manipulating them. The controversy about whether a plug should be reeled immediately when it strikes the water or allowed to rest a moment before reeling, in order to allay the fish's suspicions, is not quite so important as deciding for all time what sort of manipulation of your plug brings out its most attractive qualities for game fish.

Most people reel too fast. In the first place, the lure then travels too swiftly for the fish to catch up with it in case it sees it from a distance. With most lures fast reeling prevents the required action, and often brings the lure too quickly to the surface with an undesired overdisturbing movement. There is another thing to be said about this: a man who hurries his deceit in this manner seldom strikes a game fish well and, when the fish does see the lure, it also becomes apprised of the angler and the boat simultaneously.

When you do not succeed in taking bass or other game fish with a plug by the method of starting to reel it the instant it hits the water, try letting it rest and alternate slow reeling. There is good reason for this, and you may hook into big fellows when, for some cause, they are suspicious of moving objects.

Hunches toward using the still-lure method occasionally have come to me during unsuccessful fishing periods, and when I followed them—who would not follow a hunch?—I had good returns. In a Quebec lake in the region of Maniwaki one afternoon not a rise would come to the offerings of my wife and myself. She was suddenly attacked by a backlash in about thirty feet of water, while the red and gold deceit rested for a moment during the ensuing untangling maneuvers on the surface. Then came the big surprise. An enormous small-mouth bass catapulted itself at that lure and hung on, truculent.

Whatever wooden plug you feature, have confidence in it. Without confidence, you will not work out systematically all the pockets or other natural abiding places when fish are in a striking mood. No lure will do business for you when it reposes most of the time in the innermost recesses of your tackle box. Be as persistent for the likely places as a quail dog is for the game he seeks. Do not give up your hopes until you have plugged and plugged with all types and colorations of wooden lures.

Light plugs are just as effective as large ones. Small ones are made weighing one-half an ounce. They are just as alluring as the standard size, but require a slightly whippier and lighter rod to cast them effectively. Some anglers with stiff rods prefer these small plugs to such an extent that they fish with them exclusively. In order that no change of rod will be obligatory for the easy casting of their lure, they add a quarter-ounce dipsey or weighted snap swivel sinker to make up for the discrepancy in weight essential for comfortable casting with a stiff action rod.

Every imaginable sort of fresh- or salt-water game fish will strike some plug. These activities are not left solely to trout, bass, wall-eyes, muskies, northern pike or pickerel, but pollock, striped bass, sea trout, channel bass, barracuda, robalo and even sailfish will fall for the lure of these deceiving wooden images. Special large models are made for tarpon, sailfish and muskies, but all have the peculiar dive, wiggle, dart and shimmy of the ever-popular wooden plug.

CHAPTER VIII

METAL SPINNING AND DARTING BAITS

WHEN the first angler, whether some aborigine seeking food or one who had some instincts for catching fish for sport's sake alone, saw a silver-sided shiner or other minnow grabbed in the maw of a pike or other sportive fish, he decided that minnows were the right sort of bait, and, later on, finding that they were not easily obtainable, he began to think about an artificial imitation which would encourage a similar attack. Those who doubt this had best look over some of the early fishing outfits found among the Eskimos, where they will find that these people had some knowledge of artificial lures—objects of their own fabrication which would attract fish close enough to be speared or cause them to attack their contrivances and thus become affixed on a bone hook. The lure was a varicolored bone, and the line of seal hide. While we realize the utility of their creations, they were made on models which are opposed to our present ideas.

The reels were effective for winding the collected units of fine hide, the only sort of line with which they were acquainted.

I have asked a great number of northern Indians if they could tell what caused them to believe that fish would at times strike an inanimate object. An ancient Ojibwa at Pine Camp on French River told me that years ago, while spearing fish at the subsidence of a rapid, as he let the spear trail in the water, a large fish attacked one of the prongs and momentarily hung to it. Another said that he had seen "L'achigan" (bass) attack a floating leaf late one warm summer evening and this had actuated his cutting a piece of wood to resemble a minnow.

Near Kenora, on the Lake of the Woods, I questioned an old Ojibwa on the subject of artificial lures; whereat he escorted me to a camp of blueberry pickers on an island and shouted to an old, wrinkled squaw who, despite the heavy seas, was trying out a new birch bark canoe which had been recently made for her. She claimed she was a hundred years old; her hands were like bird claws, the seams in her face made it stand out in bold relief like the image on a coin. She spoke freely and related how, when a girl, she had seen

74

Indians cover minnows made of whittled wood with silver paper taken from labels and tobacco wrappings, and use them not only as decoy minnows but also, while fishing for lake trout, troll with them.

Much of past fishing history with artificial lures could be traced through the north tribes which had to make fish a great part of their menu, and the findings would prove that the glitter of inanimate things was used by them to induce their prey to strike, or at least show inquisitiveness, before the white man ever thought of it. How far back this was conceived by whites in fishing waters in Europe has been still left unwritten, but spoons and spinning baits were within the ken of the first anglers before people on this side of the water began to be acquainted with the gentle sport of angling.

Pearl shells, copper, and later nickel, silver and gold plate on metal added to the list of flashings used years ago to lure game fish, and, with the exception of the new frog, scale and other finishes, on all modern lures we find the same thing, though the metal is made to revolve in a different manner, and the shapes are quite different from the spoons or strictly blade patterns of early casting periods.

75

Bait-casting fashions call for both old and new types. Never are the old models entirely discarded, though the new are taken up with the notion that they are better attractions, whether they are or not. Probably in spoons and spinners the real line of demarcation between the old and the new, from the standpoint of anglers, is the ease of casting and functioning. The lure that casts without effort and is no great drag on the rod when being reeled, if it catches fish, invariably gets the most calls.

When it comes to the art of bait casting, it is well to call all metal revolving lures spinners. That is the way they are most frequently designated these days, though the larger sizes popular with muskellunge fishermen are usually spoons; and while some can be cast without sinkers, the extremely large sizes are very clumsy and are regarded strictly as trolling lures.

In the line of spoons and spinners we have the strictly spoon, or oval shape, some of them fluted, some of them not; also, with the hammered effect. Some are nearly round and some have the contour of a willow leaf, but narrowing at each end. The old style spinners—very good lures—are hung on a wire shank in different ways in

76

METAL SPINNING CASTING LURES

order that they may revolve and a clasp is devised
for attaching a single, double or treble bucktail
or feathered fly. The spoon's revolving radiates
the dashes and flashes of a minnow; and perhaps
the best reason for the feather attachment is the
fact that in the water it may possibly convey the
idea of the tail of a minnow, though almost every
sort of argument—all with intelligent backing—
will declare that the curiosity of the fish is aroused
by the antics of the lure and the assembled coloration of the hair or feathered trailer.

The most modern spoons and spinners are
made with ball bearings in order that they will
revolve and retrieve easily. You will find numbers who pin their faith to a single-bladed variety
and others to the tandem sort, the type which
has two blades, one in front of the other. In
some of these types, especially those with propeller blades, and close imitations of them, we find
that they are fashioned for one propeller to revolve in one direction and the other in another.

The advocates of double spinners are emphatic
in their declarations that their favorites will catch
fish, more fish than singles. Against this the
friends of the singles oppose the statement that
the former are more difficult to reel and are not

such reliable fish getters. The irrefutable facts are that the doubles are a little harder to reel but cause more flash. Their ability to rise more fish will always be a moot question with me.

Recently, with the arrival of a big following of bait casters who are very enthusiastic about the use of pork strips in bait casting, while single hooks and an ordinary single-blade spinner yet hold the attention of many anglers, specially made baits are annually seen for this purpose. Spinners—differently shaped, according to the type used by most manufacturers—are placed at the head of the bodies of metal or of an unbreakable composition. These are followed by specially arranged hooks or regular hooks for attaching the pork rind strip. In some cases the body is of plated metal, pyralin or some similar material. These bodies may be designated as minnow-shaped or not, just as they appear to the beholder. They are all nice little lures, of the proper weight, and on account of their lack of bulk always will be great favorites because they are sure to bring a strike from game fish which are around and in striking humor. Those which are equipped with feathered or bucktail trailers are used, also, with the pork rind strip. Nearly every one of these

78

baits has an action peculiarly its own and influences the pork strip accordingly. A few have no spinners at the head, only a slanting construction which effects a darting, side-to-side movement, which is really as killing as any other.

The old phantom minnow no longer is regarded as a casting bait, though it has spinning or revolving qualities. The use of too many hooks invariably caused it to pick up trash, leaves and weeds all the time. Even when weighted right, it had the bad habit of getting into all sorts of tangles, and none has yet been devised which does not require an unnecessary amount of swivels to prevent twisting of the line. Other revolving lures became so much more satisfactory that a phantom minnow is rarely seen in a strictly bait-casting kit.

Before speaking about casting spoons and spinners, it is advisable to mention an essential which is too often neglected. All blades ought to be polished bright with a little oil and a piece of cloth and be oiled where the lug rests on the bearing. This latter is necessary if you wish the lure to function easily. Look over the lugs and bearings and rid the parts of dirt, moss, bits of weeds, etc., which have gathered there during prior fishing. Even lures which have never been used ought to have the same attention, for dirt will accumulate in vital parts, however much the manufacturers strive with so much care, while packing them, to prevent it. Then, too, they have to contend with the human element while in the process of making. Often enamel, as well as paint and plating, drops on the bearings, and this will be certain to slow up the revolving movement unless remedied.

This is especially true of the spinners that are at the front of feather lures, which are made together and are not detachable. The bait-casting spinning, bucktail flies, feather flies and bait-casting feather minnows should have their blades kept clean and all extraneous matter removed in order that they will perform without a drag of any kind.

If you are fishing downstream fast water, things will go easily for you whether wading or moving in a boat. Cast toward the banks, logs, rocks and other likely places, but start your bait moving the instant it touches the water. When you permit a revolving bait to become inactive, it has no luring qualities and is very likely to hook itself on something beneath the surface which may cause you to lose it. A moving spinner is not in so much danger, and it becomes attractive the instant its blade, or blades, starts to revolve.

Usually upstream fishing is resultless, or at least very trying, on account of the necessity of reeling so speedily to prevent the bait from becoming inactive. In lots of places with the fastest reeling, it is almost impossible to prevent this. Accuracy in casting, however, has an opportunity of showing its worth. If the bait caster is sufficiently skilled to drop his lure in the upstream currents which are everywhere present in fast waters, he will find it worth while. Moreover, behind the big rocks and obstructions amidstream, although some angling authorities say it is useless to cast there, large trout and small-mouthed bass frequently lurk and, when they happen to be there, look out for a large one and a prompt, rough battle.

The majority of anglers reel altogether too fast both in rapid and calm water. Do not try to speed up so long as the blades are revolving though ever so slowly. Impart an occasional jerk to the rod in order to simulate the quick sideways turn of a frightened minnow. This often produces an attack from bass when seemingly they are inactive.

When a bass strikes and misses, slow up your reeling, but do not stop altogether while viewing the spectacle, as many do. Even if you only keep the spoon or spinner blade revolving leisurely, that fish is likely to hit it again before it is returned to you, particularly if he has not seen you. Fish often follow the spinner closely out of curiosity, not showing the least intention to hit it. Once in a while a jerky act on your part quickly changes the movement and causes a recalcitrant finny warrior to attack, though at first all that actuated him was the sole pleasure of witnessing its colorations and movements.

Spinners and spoons can be fished as surface baits and soon prove their value. When in weed beds, game fish may be several feet away from the edge in places where it is impossible to cast without becoming fouled in weeds, moss, or an undergrowth. These do not insure the movement of the spinners. Something out of the ordinary must attract the fish to an open place where the spinners are doing their best to disport in a minnow-like fashion. Hold the rod high in your left hand so that the spinner blades will continue to revolve at the surface and create a fussy disturbance in the water. Fish will become attracted and dart out to seize the bait, though a silent lure would not have urged them.

The first wobbling or darting types of spoons were designed for trolling. Bait casters observed their luring qualities and promptly urged manufacturers to make them in regular casting weights and sizes compatible with their sport; and response came in the form of those now on the market designed for the wielders of the short rods and multiplying reels. These lures are made of one piece of metal, shaped so that when reeled they dart from side to side, wiggle, half roll, or otherwise show considerable resemblance to a live minnow. They actually revolve in fast water or when reeled briskly, but this is not so much desired as their wobbling antics.

The forms in which they come are various; they resemble a shoe horn, a fish or some oval object. The water resistance occurs in the bend or twist, thus creating their luring qualities. As they are made in all sizes, their adaptability is perfect for anything from a small trout to a tarpon. Having practically no wind resistance they clear their way in a veritable gale, though a large wooden lure, in such conditions, seldom drops with the accuracy of the angler's intent. The wobblers have their faults—the least bit of trash attaching on their trailer hooks kills their action and they are tough customers to reel against current. Fast water causes them to revolve and twist lines badly, but this can be avoided to a great extent by the use of barrel swivels. Snap swivels prevent the line from twisting, but they destroy some of the potency of the lure. All of the wobblers give best results when reeled slowly, for they act like a lazy shiner, whether the finish is copper, silver, gold, frog (the present-day ubiquitous scale finish) or any coloration.

CHAPTER IX

A LITTLE BASS KNOWLEDGE

WHAT part large- and small-mouth bass had in establishing the art of bait casting as a permanent sport is easy to estimate from the amount of tackle specially made for them and the unalterable fact that the entire popularity of the sport at its present stage is due chiefly to these game fishes. All the angling paraphernalia used in bait casting had the bass family to develop it. The standard of this pastime is invariably measured by this fish, and what, in the same manner, is achieved for pike and other fishes with few exceptions had its original test among the bronze-backs.

There are two reasons for bass being regarded as correlative with the progress of bait casting. In the first place, bass respond more quickly to artificial lures than any other game fish; then, they are more widely distributed and more plentiful than pike, trout or muskellunge. And we ought to add, too, to this statement, the fact that they strike more throughout the season and oftener during the day than any other fish we know of, though, we admit, they are temperamental at times and are prone to vary their habits in this respect.

So many suggestions regarding the origin of artificial lures have been offered to anglers of the present day that it is but just to recognize all of them as having merit, yet remembering that particular localities had a part to play with all of them. We will only state that the first dyed-in-the-wool fisherman, who saw a bass strike some object, animate or inanimate, on the surface of a lake or stream, immediately was seized by a desire to take one of them, at some future period, with some creation of his own resembling what he saw the bronze warriors attack so viciously.

Bass have been seen to strike a still object, moved not in the least by wind or wave. They literally exploded after it with all the noise and surrounding disturbance of a rocket. These acts seemed to have a great deal of sportiveness.

When a boy, before the bait-casting fever held sway, I often observed bass following and striking a moving object and just as frequently saw them follow it, as though to strike, and stop at the very instant when they appeared ready to seize it. This proved that only when close did they realize it was only a deceit—a mere resemblance to something they had in mind which they wanted.

I recall when deer hunting one warm fall, years ago, in the Ozarks, while waiting on a stand at the head of Brushy Creek, that an incident brought to my mind a possibility of taking bass by artificial means, especially of the wooden-minnow variety. Inadvertently dropping a small piece of bark in the water, I saw a bass rise, seize it and fling it out of its mouth with apparently one action. Forthwith, being interested, I dropped many such sticks and small pieces of bark and procured similar responses. Deer hunting momentarily escaped my mind. Presently I cut a minnow-shaped piece of bark and tied a string to it. After adding a piece of gravel for a weight and tying it to a willow limb, I drew it slowly beneath the water. Fish suddenly started for it. These little bass immediately presented a picture of what later occurred when they were in a striking mood and a wooden replica of a live minnow appeared and swam within their range of vision.

Why bass strike lures is a question which has puzzled many a writer on angling subjects, chiefly because at times they attack any moving object resembling something upon which they feed or which inhabits water and its environments, and, at other times, they scrutinize most carefully any bait which is offered them, however strongly it bears similitude to natural minnows, frogs and insects of various kinds. A single experience might give the reader an idea why so many writers never seem to explain well the cause of a bass's animosity toward, or a penchant for, certain things.

I was casting for a large bass which in an exceedingly clear river I had seen seek a crypt under an overhanging bank. As I was fifty feet away, I could not tell whether he saw me or not. At least, he gave no sign of it, if he did. Numerous times I cast right at him, above, to one side, a few feet in front, with a wooden minnow, then with several variations of models, and in all the colorations which manufacturers have fabricated —rainbow, white and red, scale finish—the entire range of tints and nuances. Not a movement did he accord me. Then I tried my best to procure a response with feathered flies of minnow shape, casting spinners with bucktail trailers, and, finally, two pork rind minnows of much repute.

That phlegmatic bass paid not the least attention to a single one of them; and they might not have existed in his lurking place, so far as he showed any interest. After a time, for the fun of the incongruous presentation, I attached to my line an old type wooden surface lure which had been in my tackle box for years. My results with it had been so poor that for a long time it had remained in a small isolated receptacle until it had no more paint on it and its hooks were very rusty. This I cast to that bass. It dropped upside down and had no more movement in the water than an inert, small piece of ordinary wood. Yet instantly the bass struck and hung on to it.

At another time, the behavior of a bass surprised me as much as this one. I was fly-fishing for a similar fish which I had marked lying at the side of a sycamore log. I tried flies of many names and colors, fly-rod lures looking like minnows, and finally a live minnow that I followed with a frog. Not a motion, not a rise, came from Mr. Micropterus. The instant I began to retrieve my live minnow from the water a walnut fell on the water from a tree on the bank above. With the speed of lightning, that big bass struck it, knocking it almost on to the shore, then he swam angrily for the deep water.

With all the explanations offered regarding the striking characteristics of bass, and what actuates them, we feel we can say with assurance that no one particular mood or mental state alone encourages it, but almost all of them which are included in the repertoire composed of hunger, anger, jealousy, play, curiosity, and natural, unbridled belligerence towards any shape of invader near or within its presumed lair. This latter trait really is the one which explains why a small-mouth bass will not only seize a small live minnow but will also attack a predacious fish greatly its superior in size and weight.

The two species of bass which anglers are most eager to meet are the large-mouth and small-mouth varieties. Frequently we find the two living in the same lake or river in the North Country or in the northern part of the United States. But in the southern part of the United States, the fighting small-mouths are found only in the cold hill streams of fast water, either alone or in the company of large-mouths. Except in a few private lakes—spring-fed—small-mouths are not native to southern lakes, though their cousins, the large-mouths, seem to thrive abundantly in all of them. Small-mouths are found as far south as northern Alabama and Georgia, and a few fast waters that spill out of the hills of southern Arkansas into northern Louisiana. The last statement has been questioned, but the veracity of it has been sustained by a personal visit.

In casting for different varieties of bass and in various places so removed from each other that the habits of the fish differ at times, the best asset is the knowledge derived from study of the locality and constant experimenting with lures at all hours of the day. Simply because a man declares that he has not had any success in a particular water with a certain lure does not mean that it has no effect there. He may not have given it sufficient opportunities to perform, and we know that wind and weather, heat and cold, may have affected the taste of the bass family for investigating artificial lures, whatever their colorations or shapes. In fact, there are quite a few waters which are said to hold families of only unresponsive bass, because they have been sought at only certain hours and with only certain methods. I am firm in my belief that, no matter where they are, bass at some time will strike artificial lures, though the time and the lure have to be discovered, as well as something about the environs.

I recall two waters which were supposed never to have yielded bass to the casting artistry of a single angler who used artificial bait. One is very close to a large city in Michigan—an abandoned rock quarry filled with crystal blue, transparent water which is plentifully stocked with small-mouths. The other is a vast spread of water in Ontario studded with islands and known as Lake Penage. The quarry pond was a puzzler to me at first, for it refused to bring a single rise. The bigger lake needed only investigation and common sense applied to it, where casting should be practiced, as well as how.

When the quarry pond had my attention, despite the unanimous evidence of all local anglers that no fish had ever been known to grab at anything but live bait, I yet regarded it as a good prospective for indulging in casting for bass profitably. What brought this about was merely observing that there were no trees about to make shady lurking places. There were no shallows anywhere, so bass which waited for prey near the surface must be close to, or under, the shelving rock, and the least noise or movement along the shore line of such a small body of water would be bound to transmit vibrations of announcement of an enemy's presence to the small-mouths.

Day hardly appeared when I made my first venture. Not a human being was about. I stood far from any rocky shore and cast into the opposite pocket. The instant that wobbling plug struck, the water literally boiled with bass as numbers tried to seize it. My initial cast brought the first small-mouth which was ever caught with a man-made lure in that miniature lake.

Now I am prone to recall Lake Penage at the time I first visited it, and the uncomplimentary remarks of an angler made after the writer referred him to it and he caught no bass, forthwith announcing that it was an impossibility for any angler to take bass there with any fly-rod lure. Most of the information provided me by visiting anglers was to the effect that it was useless to try to take bass with inanimate lures of any sort. Minnows and worms were the only things which brought bass to the camp frying pan. And still I was not convinced that I would err if I persisted in fishing my favorite way. All the casters who had failed invariably had gone to the parts where their guides had directed and these were located where only still fishermen had success. Furthermore, bass would not resort to the shallow rocky places where they ought to strike best until the prevailing high winds died down late in the evening or when the water was calm in the morning, save for a rippling disturbance. Another thing which might affect the sport of casting, I reflected, was a quick change to cold weather.

The first day proved that the foundation of my scheme for success was based on a bit of piscatorial foreknowledge. I fished close to camp, casting from a boat precisely in the parts where the recognized local and visiting experts with live bait would never think of trying. In a single hour I took the legal limit and, except during two cold days, when hard winds were blowing, I always succeeded in reaching the legal daily limit of bass in a short time.

The reason I refer to these two places and the incidents connected with them is that there is a likelihood of the same things prevailing in other places which I have never visited. Nothing deters a beginner like the lack of success. And he may persistently fish a bad locality in waters teeming with fish because his guide caused him to cast in parts where he knows bait fishermen have

94

achieved good results, and from lack of success give up the sport of casting before he has tried it in the very parts where it ought to have been pursued.

All of this is applicable to the South as much as the North. Every stream, lake or pond, wherever it happens to be, has its peculiarities. If you are convinced that bass are there, do not jump at conclusions that they cannot be taken *via* the casting art, if they do not rise during your first few trials. Study the water itself, the shore line, the logs or stumps of trees in the water, the wind and the weather. Finally, put together all your theories and eliminate one after the other until you find the true cause of your failure. After that, you will be able to put in your angling records more accounts of the capture of nice fish than any of barren bait-casting days. Remember, too, if time hangs heavy on your hands during periods when fish are not striking, you can enjoy practice casting. This will give you almost as much pleasure as the taking of fish, and, at the same time, sharpen your eye, train your thumb, and cause your wrist to function almost automatically.

CHAPTER X

BAIT CASTING FOR BASS

WE cannot lay too great stress on the importance of gaining some knowledge of the lakes and streams which you are about to fish. The reason this is repeated so often is that there are many local causes which have apparently a sinister effect on the fishing. A little information gathered here and there frequently puts the angler on his guard and saves him from wasting valuable hours in barren parts or during periods when the water is affected to such a degree that it has influence on the sport of casting quite contrary to what is desired. Nevertheless, there are thousands of anglers who chafe with impatience when unoccupied and take huge delight in studying what is preventing the fish from striking and discovering the best places for resultful casting.

I have to recall my own experiences, and how they broadened my angling conceptions about localities through many trips into heretofore unknown parts. In the few mountain streams where

96

I first did any casting with artificial lures, the waters were of almost unbelievable clarity. If at any time they were made the least murky—to the degree that anything in a depth of six to ten feet was not plainly visible—it was useless to cast any lure.

This was, and still is, an unalterable fact, though purely a local condition. The first time I ever saw the Upper Mississippi, the Saint Croix, and others, I hesitated about fishing them. The clear water at home surpassed these at their normal and low stages so much that it was difficult for me to realize that the fishing in these northern parts was not affected by a freshet and that the waters were in a fit state for casting. And, while I have visited the northern streams and lakes for a number of years and now know I am wrong, every time I come to the above-mentioned waters, the same impression as on my first visit prevails; but, naturally, I pay no attention to it.

The reason I state this is that it has done more than all else to disappoint anglers about waters because, when they arrived, fish were not striking and on this account they felt sure that there were no game fish there. Particularly is this true when

97

waters are blooming. This is a condition prevailing mostly in the northern states when the moss and aqueous plants and similar still life around are in bloom. The water seems to hold in suspension small particles of tiny green or other colored matter, a sort of sediment resembling pulverized paint. In thousands of lakes, bass will not strike artificial lures when these periods occur, though in deep water they will respond to the user of homely live baits. There is only one thing to do then—wait, or seek the parts of the body of water where, on account of the direction of the wind, vegetation is not so prevalent. Often, in parts of a big lake, however, where there is no wind, certain regions are free from it.

As in other fishing, bait casting brings greatest success to the man who uses the utmost precaution against creating any disturbances. When on the subject of bass fishing, some may take issue with me on this point and vociferously declare that some anglers catch their largest bass when their lure falls on the water with a resounding splash. This is not as often true as when their movements are most guarded, and there is only an occasional exception, just as some men have success by letting their lure rest a few minutes on the surface before they start reeling it in, while the reverse for the majority apparently brings best results nearly every time.

If wading a stream, remember that care is even more necessary than when in a boat. Fish downstream and cast toward the bank. Bass are frightened more quickly than trout and remain suspicious of man's advent longer than the beautiful redspots. A great deal of study must be given all streams which are not too deep to wade or afford places here and there to send lures to likely places. It is possible to fish slow streams against the flow. Swift waters need forethought and the application of fishing knowledge, because, frequently, they cannot be waded and here and there conditions arise which force them to be fished upstream.

Naturally, there is a necessary expertness to be acquired for upstream fishing and other things are to be considered, however likely the spot where you wish to place your lure. In quick water, however fast you are reeling, the current promptly kills the action of the bait, and you have to work fast to keep it from lodging on the bottom against some sunken rock or log. There is only one place to cast, and that is in the eddies and upstream currents, and while your lure is in them it performs every action you wish. Often some fine game fish like to stay in such places to feed, and, obviously, while they are in such places for food they will attack anything which invades their lair.

Floating down river in a boat or canoe is a popular form of indulging in the sport of bait casting. It is such a silent, stealthy approach that you reach the lair of the game fish without their being apprised of it. Learn to cast while sitting. In swift water, the least touch of the craft against a log, rock or shallow piece of bar is likely to make you lose your balance and fall in the water. Furthermore, when seated, you are not so likely to forewarn bass of your presence. Also, when seated, your boatman or paddler can see ahead of you any obstacles in his way. Cast with the wrist and over-the-shoulder method toward the bank and, in very swift water, at an angle of thirty degrees in advance. By the time the lure drops and you start reeling, the lure will be in a straight line from you and, by the time you recover it, you will be reeling it in from an angle of forty-five degrees or more.

In many good fishing localities, it will be necessary to cast sideways with the wrist movement on account of overhanging limbs. It is always advisable to get as far under them as possible, as they are the very places to which bass resort to wait for their prey. Obviously, if here you practiced the over-the-shoulder style of casting you would be continually hanging your lures in the trees instead of under them.

Fast water provides an excellent opportunity for mastering the silent cast, a most effective method, especially when bass are exceedingly wary and take fright easily. Practice it and you will learn just the precise moment to stop the reel with your thumb and thus prevent a noisy splash.

Be sure to start your lure the instant it alights, and while transferring the rod to your left hand, if, instead of pointing your rod tip directly toward the lure while making your recovery, you elevate it partially, as I have advised for dry-line fishing, you will almost unconsciously hook your fish without any extra effort. In fact, the fish, against the spring of the rod, hooks himself very frequently.

A mere touch of the wrist is sufficient to set the hook in any of your strikes from bass. Yet, every year, we see hundreds of anglers setting the hook with all the muscular force at their command.

Not infrequently, they tear the hooks out of the mouths of their intended prey, or cause such a rip that the instant the fish leaps and shakes itself vigorously the hook is easily ejected and freedom is obtained.

In time, with experience, the bait-casting rod becomes so responsive in the hands of an angler that his accuracy in shooting a lure may well be called deadly. But in fishing there are other needs than actual casting while manipulating a rod. An angler should know how, by a gentle touch, he can avoid a rock or make his lure jump a log, or prevent its lodging in a tree without having to pull it back violently and dangerously and, if nothing else, encourage a badly tangled line. Moreover, such skill can be successfully employed in maneuvering a strong fish away from dangerous obstacles. Often a mere touch does it, whereas if you apply all your strength the fish seems all the more determined to reach such a possible source of safety. A good way to practice this is with a wooden lure, because then there is no danger of losing it if an unexpected backlash occurs, or swift water or anything else causes you to lose your mastery momentarily.

In lake or stream, continually visualize fish and

all the possible places which might harbor bass. Cast close to them and never overlook any. Cover one mile a day well instead of covering haphazardly fifteen. After a few fishing trips, the angler will know what places it is useless to fish.

While you can lay down no infallible rules, there are many things worth constant observation. The main one, a summarization, is to keep out of sight. Another is to cast toward the likely places. Indications of the presence of bass will be distinguished by the close observer, particularly so when they are rising to insects or making life miserable for schools of minnows. They feed on almost every variety of the latter and usually when they are feeding near the surface bass can be depended upon to strike artificial lures.

Never overlook weed beds or lily pads, however shallow the water. There is ample concealment there for the fish. Often they are quite far back and do not get sight of a lure cast toward the edge. Then, obviously, the silent cast is not so effective. Do not be afraid to let your lure drop with a loud splash. And if it is the type which splutters a great deal when being reeled, so much the better. You have to attract the attention of the fish somehow. Frequently, they will come a long way out of weeds to find out what has happened. If, by chance, they happen to get a glimpse of some object which appears to resemble a minnow, frog or other tidbit, they are sure to make a determined effort to get it with their big mouths.

Many anglers pay no attention to casting toward sheer rocky bluffs where deep water is known to be. This is not a good policy. Often, just under the water, are shelves and benches of rock where bass stay for a chance at their rightful prey. Some of the largest small-mouths I ever saw taken were brought to rise in just such places. There is nothing more spectacular than to see a bass coming with a rush from ten or twenty feet of water to smash at a surface lure. Veritably, in his unbridled abandon, he seems to be imbued with the idea that momentarily he wants to see how far he can knock it out of the water and, at the same time, display his magnificent bronze physique.

I have often asked anglers why they were so partial to surface lures when the fish, in the waters they were fishing, responded better to semi-underwater lures and standard underwater lures. Always the answer was that the sight of a single fish striking a surface lure appealed to them more than hundreds hooked beneath the surface.

Rocky indentations are favorite places for bass, particularly if they are not too deep. There are many favorable hiding places for them in what often appear at first glance to be shallow water and sandy stretches devoid of vegetation. Often sunken logs, half sandcovered and submerged, harbor a bass. Then, too, there are circular holes and similar holes which are quite worthy of the versatile caster's attentions. These are perhaps screened by mossy growths but it makes them none the less attractive. If I were to fish shoals regularly, it would be very early in the morning or late in the evening and I would approach all favorable places very stealthily and make the most of being able to cast distances of seventy-five feet and more.

Fast rivers merit considerable study before the best of fishing is obtained. So many run by the favorite places of bass without bestowing the slightest attention upon them. Rocks amidstream, logs merely semi-submerged, the brawling water at the foot of falls, swift, wild, white water concealing sharp-toothed bowlders and upstream swirls always furnish good small-mouth bass, as well as fighting grounds of sufficiently perilous character to augment the piquancy of the sport. And bass like gravel and hard clay banks, though from a distance the territory might not appear favorable. Still they stay in the cut-in banks and holes made by the swirling current, for they know these are places that will provide them bounteously with food. Never neglect banks anywhere that are overhung by trees or otherwise shaded, particularly during hot days when bass are thought to be down, lethargic, in deep water, and temporarily uninterested in things animated or the reverse.

The best fishing condition of water is when there is a nice ripple and no strong winds are blowing. Of two shores, both of similar character, select the one against which the wind is beating. Usually, it is the more productive, though not necessarily so in all cases. Lakes have this advantage over fast rivers: they are more dependable for fishing because they are not so easily affected by freshets, though the belligerent qualities of fast water bass transcend those of lake bass. However, it must not be forgotten that their habitat aids them in putting up a better fight against the bait caster's equipment.

The question has often been raised about the respective merits of underwater, semi-underwater and surface lures. We are not bold enough to say that one variety is better than another at all times, but rather express ourselves with the modification that one seems to surpass another under specific conditions. All of them own wonderful potentialities for fish taking. Taking the matter bit by bit, the best way of making a universal declaration is by stating that when bass are down in fairly deep water the strictly underwater lures are the most successful; when they are striking near the surface, pin your faith to the semi-underwater. When nothing seems to attract them except something on the surface, the surface type ought to have your first choice. Then remember that all these reverse themselves, for bass promptly change their deportment so quickly that an experienced bait caster must have a versatile supply of lures to be ready for any emergency of this sort.

Night fighting requires for best results strictly surface baits. The darker the color and the darker the night, you will have more big fish strike. Nevertheless, nite-luming baits are very popular with many anglers. They are finished with one of the night-luming pigments and have good records to their credit. All who use them should expose them to sunlight; otherwise, their coloration will not be so efficacious. Obviously, acquaintance with a lake or stream is an asset in night casting for you will avoid many bad places which would be only trouble makers, though there are usually plenty of striking fish amongst them. All light should be out—not even a darkened lantern is permitted among night casters. Usually they depend only on a handy flashlight when they are landing their fish. You have to strike and reel the instant you hear a fish smash or it will eject your lure faster than you ever believed possible.

Even expert fishermen use antibacklash reels when casting at night. It is no joke to have to untangle a backlash by the aid of a mere flashlight. Then, too, the thumb will play truant at night, though in the daytime it is ever so accurate. Some antibacklash reels are equipped with a bail in addition to the friction device, which prevents their overrunning after the lure strikes the water. With ordinary reels conjecture must be indulged in and when it goes awry a backlash has been started for the next time you attempt a long cast.

All surface lures at night need to be reeled very slowly, in a jerky fashion, stopping and starting while Mr. Micropterus decides whether to fling himself at it or not. All types seemingly get fish. The spluttering they produce which attracts fish is caused either by a grooved head, a metal piece affixed for the same purpose, or spinners at each end of lures of wood so light that it will not submerge. But fish go for underwater lures, too, at night. They are not, however, so popular, as anglers lose too many fish when they are not able to discover where such an object is traveling.

Expertness in landing bass is almost as important as efficient casting skill. Advice of value here is simple, yet it ought to be meticulously followed until your actions become second nature with you the instant you realize your fish is hooked. First, look over your battle ground. Steer, if possible, away from the logs, rocks, submerged trees and innumerable other things to which a fish will dart to escape its barbed captor. It is second nature for bass to seek refuge where the most dangers to tackle exist. Only let your fish bore deep when you are positive nothing awaits there to aid it in parting from your hook. A bass is the most resourceful and versatile of all game fish. Its flights above water cannot be anticipated with accuracy, for it will vary the frequency of its jumping against all your anticipations. Let a strong fish run where no dangers exist, but never give it the least appreciable slack, nor exert too much strength so that you will help it tear the hook from its mouth. Deftness is essential and worthy of cultivation.

Fast water bass are never landed until they are in the boat, canoe or creel. They will resort to a variety of aërial flights and unexpected subaqueous plunges. Then, in the swiftest parts where they live, they will lie broadside and permit the entire force of the current to strike their broad flanks. Under such circumstances, there is no hope of reeling against it and the only thing to do is to work them into quiet water, then you can coax them close to the boat or the shore, and land them with your fingers in their mouth, a much more satisfactory method for a lone bait caster than with a landing net.

The man who depends on a heavy strong line and stiff rod, who reels the fish in by sheer force, will never get much sport out of bait casting.

BAIT CASTING FOR BASS

Light tackle, fine lines and willingness to give the fish at all times the same chances for freedom as in fly-fishing are what constitute a truly ethical bait caster for bass.

CHAPTER XI

BAIT CASTING FOR LARGE TROUT

A FEW years ago, the writer would have been surprised if an angler so much as intimated that a brook, rainbow or brown trout would change his usual deportment by flinging himself at any sort of an artificial lure.

This brief method of introduction recalls an incident of recent date. The setting was the most famous brook trout stream in the world. It went to prove that many angling traditions die hard, so much so that the one about whom I am writing now would not admit as real what he had seen, as though it had all been but a momentary fantastic vision effected by some trickery flashed before his eyes.

At the resort near the big fast stream which I was fishing an English angler had spent a week, trying the river everywhere in its entire length of forty-five miles which seemed to offer a harboring place for brook trout. That he was a dry-fly artist from first to last was palpable from his rod to his leader, and the contents of his well-stocked fly book. He declared that he had whipped resultlessly every part of the river without any acknowledgment from the redspots. So futile had been his casting that he fully believed that there was not a trout in the stream. All the publicity bestowed upon it had its origin in the brains of the resort owners, he believed. No one feels in the best of spirits when he has crossed the Big Pond especially for a try at record' trout and never received a rise.

I wanted to help and offered my services. While he was much taken aback when I informed him that these trout would not look at twelves, fourteens or sixteens—however well made or great the variety of the creations—and that they preferred large floating or underwater bass-size flies; when I described bait casting for trout and insisted upon its practicability, he calmly examined me unbelievingly through his glasses. And the farther I progressed in my recital the less he believed me, though he was pretty well shocked when I told him that he could dry-fly fish from one end of the river to the other with his tiny Hare's Ears, March Browns and other pets without getting a single big trout.

Finally I was emboldened to ask him to accompany me to the stream where I showed him a bait I had had constructed for casting with a bait-casting rod for large trout. It was an ordinary bass-size feather minnow in a Silver Doctor pattern, but, instead of the usual cork body, it had a quarter-ounce lead one and a spinner in front near the eye of the 1/0 Model Perfect hook. In his eyes, what an atrocity, what a lure with which to attempt, by the strangest flight of the imagination, to catch a game fish! Smilingly he agreed to my importunities to witness a trial. Doubt warred with his piscatorial experience. But the only way, I am sure, that I ever had him momentarily interested, was through his desire to see in what manner I flung any distance from me that impossible bait.

I cast the lure a hundred feet away and recovered it through the vehement waters. Again I cast and midway of the first distance, while on the retrieve, in the swiftest part, I hooked on to a four-pound brook trout. Then the fight was on, with the whippy rod, while the rushing current aided the fish for a time during its incessant, militant resistance. Finally I landed the fish before the unbelieving eyes of a British subject. For a while he said nothing as we sauntered back to camp, though his eyes never left the big trout. I questioned him for a time without reply, but in the end he mumbled grudgingly: "Yes, you did catch a trout with that big bait, but I cannot believe it!"

What is the explanation for a rainbow or brook trout striking an artificial lure? Simplicity itself, according to my idea. The flash of a moving object gives the impression that it is created by a minnow or something similar.

Big brook trout are avid minnow feeders. In the North Country the largest brook trout on record, fourteen and one-half pounds, was taken still fishing with a homely cockatouche as the temptation. Large trout take minnows, frogs and crayfish. They devour young pike and large pike devour trout in turn—many of them. I have caught brook trout four pounds and over literally spilling minnows. Last summer, at the Isle of Saint Ignace, I caught a seven-pound brook trout which was so full of little white shiners that there did not seem room for another; and yet, this big, red-spotted valiant struck viciously a large metal wobbling casting lure. Furthermore, in clear water I have seen a brook trout not over nine inches in length connect with a treble-hooked spoon of large muskellunge size, an outfit which had been rigged for immense great northern pike inhabiting an adjacent lake. By chance, for practice, it was flung into the little clear tributary where the canoe rested. Yet this watercourse, teeming with brook trout, had not produced a one for the fly fisherman in the party.

For quite a while I sincerely believed that I was the sole and only originator or discoverer of the sport of bait casting for trout, simply because I had seen no one else do it or heard of it from other lips. But, finally I was convinced about my mistake, as there seeped into my system the information that others had been doing it long before I ever thought it feasible. One day, on a trout stream far away from the usual trek of tourists, the redspots refused to rise, and my worthy Cree companion suggested that I use my bait-casting outfit. Then, afterwards, without any intimation on my part that I knew anything about the sport, carefully I drew from others the fact that they had pursued trout in that manner for ever so long.

Numbers now take lake trout by the same method, namely, bait casting. Why not? For years previous, the idea must have lodged in the innermost recesses of their brains when they trolled for lakers and landlocked salmon, or when they cajoled themselves into believing they were fly-fishing during long periods when they used phantom minnows and spinners for these two varieties. Lakers strike well for the bait caster in fall and spring. My first cast for lakers brought a fast-fighting landlocked salmon. Then my next attempt shifted to the north shore of Lake Superior in the region of Rossport, Ontario.

The big boys, just after the ice went out, were coming into the shoals after their favorite white, silver-sided shiners, and forthwith I promptly affixed a white-feather bait-casting minnow and proceeded to cast at random. My initial cast resulted in sufficient fish for that day. I hooked on to one of unexpected size. It was a good thing I had ample reserve line on my reel. For a while it all appeared as though I were hooked into a fast moving freight train. Straightway for deep water he rushed with my lure, oblivious of the fact that there might be a limit to my store of silk casting line and my concern for the lightness of my tackle. I won. But at what a cost of waiting and physical grief!

If you ever hang on to a twenty-pound lake trout in cold Lake Superior waters, you will better be able to appreciate the various emotions which I experienced.

That is afforded by bait casting for lake trout in early spring and late fall; no other time of the year is worth while trying. You become almost cloyed with the unexpected. When you think your results will comprise the capture of a two- or three-pounder, fate decrees that one of about twenty pounds swims away with one of your favorite lures. Conjure big fish as your sole anticipation and small chaps usually are your reward. But I am arguing only from my personal experience. Other anglers have a habit of proving that in this respect I am not immune to lake trout fallacies.

With spinners, I like the trailer, whether it is a white feathered fly or bucktail, to be tied on a No. 1 or 1/o Model Perfect hook. I like these hooks better than any other for this purpose; if you have to rough a big fish they stand the strain well. The small-sized plugs or wooden minnows are excellent lures, too, particularly those of the scale finish and white and red head. When you think they do not travel sufficiently deep add a

118

weighted snap swivel or dipsey sinker. Of late, one has appeared on the market with a grooved metal head which is a deep diver and surely gets results with the lakers.

When you hook on to a big lake trout, do not attempt to stop him as he makes his heedless run for deep water. With ordinary tackle, you could not if you wished, without suffering breakage somewhere. Let him go, and, when you feel a lull, start fighting tactics. Ultimately, you will be able to land your captive.

A variety of lures for bait casting for brook and rainbow trout offers itself—a gamut between flies of every sort, many-shaped spoons and spinners, phantom minnows, wooden plugs, bass bugs and the versatile modern feather minnow. I have several favorites. A great outfit is not required while casting for brook trout, though the angler ought to be supplied with many colors of lures in order that he will be able to cope with the temporary preferences in that respect of his favorite fish.

The little wooden plugs created for fly-rod use are exceedingly adaptable to bait casting for brook trout. Use them with weighted snap swivel sinkers or one of the lead sinkers with the wire contraption which makes it easy to fasten them to lures. Always augment this with a swivel attached to the lure. If you do not, much of the minnow-like action will be lost or it will turn over badly in swift water and twist the line. The same advice ought to be observed when using feather minnows and bass bugs. Give the preference to the latter when tied on straight-eyed hooks. The turn-down-eyed hooks are an abomination while bait casting. After heating a turn-down eye for an instant with a match, straighten it out with your pliers—which ought to be in every tackle kit. Do not attempt to straighten it until you have applied heat because most of the high-grade hooks are brittle.

Fortunately, feather minnows now come made purposely for bait casting. A lead body painted correctly takes the place of the cork body, and they have a metal spinner at the head of the proper size. You need, of them, only these patterns: Silver Doctor, Babcock, Ozark Ripley, and Shiner. Some manufacturers have other names for these standard patterns, but you can be guided in your choice by the color ensemble. A little extra enticement is accorded them when you attach a short strip of pork rind to any feathered bait. Results assure me that this addition is worth while. My judgment explains that it conveys the impression to the fish of an overeager minnow desperately following the feathered tidbit.

Spinners with bucktail and feathered flies can be used just like the feather minnows and bass bugs, but my own catches have not been so great with them; I have always been more fortunate with big trout when I used the shoehorn shaped wobbling spoons without any feather or pork rind attachment. A swivel should be connected to them; otherwise, they will twist themselves off the line in a very short time. One can hardly appreciate how many of these lures are lost by failing to provide them with swivels.

You will have more success casting for large trout in big, bowlder-strewn rivers. In small streams, the tiniest lures are required, and, necessarily, the lightest and whippiest of rods, in order to be able to cast them. The reels, too, must be fast. Any other sort of reel is a serious handicap. In wide waters, some of your best catches will come from behind big rocks in midstream in deep, swift water, though you can never tell in advance from just where your virile trout will come. Sometimes the trout will follow the lure all the way to the bank before striking it, and sometimes hit it immediately. They are not, however, so prone to do the latter and often miss numbers of attempts to seize your lure. Usually they do not strike with the abandon of a bass, nor are they so swift and accurate. Then, perhaps, an odd one will come along and give you the impression that he, at least, is just as fast and accurate as a bass.

Nevertheless, you should anticipate the habits of large trout. Reel slowly. If one misses, wait a while and again cast where he has disappeared or whence he came. Usually he will try again after a time, though he has seen you—very unlike a bass.

Often, when you have hooked a big brook trout or rainbow on a casting lure, you have him hooked to stay, despite the flouncing of the redspot or the salmon-like leaps of Mr. Irideus. The hook does not tear from their mouths so easily as from those of small-mouth bass, nor does either show the resourcefulness, in swift water, in ejecting the lure or taking advantage of every bit of fast water to help them get rid of an angler's torments. Nevertheless, when a trout bores, he has a habit of getting behind big rocks and holding there, as though he were equipped with some suction apparatus which aids him in retaining his position tenaciously.

Three of the largest brook trout I have ever seen caught by a bait caster were taken, one at midday with the sun straight overhead and two in the afternoon while the sun was shining brightly between three and four o'clock.

I saw a lady take one while bait casting in a big, crystal clear stream with a Babcock feather minnow. The fish hit close to shore and would easily have weighed six pounds. My own experience has brought my best trout very early in the morning and after sunset. The best thing about bait casting for brook and rainbow trout is that you are seldom bothered with fish weighing under a pound. Fancy a five-pounder, on a light bait casting rod, striking a hundred or a hundred and twenty-five feet away from you, and you can well appreciate that you are enjoying thrills never experienced by dry-fly casters, because real bait-casting skill for trout exacts more expertness and time to acquire it than any sort of casting with a fly rod.

CHAPTER XII

BAIT CASTING FOR MUSKIES, WALL-EYES AND PIKE

IT is no new information to a great many anglers that most of the sharp-toothed, long-muzzled, preying fish of fresh water lakes and rivers are called correctly or incorrectly "pike" and when you get down South they are all bunched under the classification of "Jacks." This applies to the true pickerel, the wall-eyed pike, called "pickerel" in the North, the great northern pike and the well-known tiger of inland waters, the muskellunge. Their interest to bait casters lies in the fact that at times they will strike every sort of artificial lure made, no matter what the coloring, the shape or the action.

Under all circumstances, I would not call the true pickerel the best fighting fish in the world, but in certain waters occasionally I have seen pickerel battle with fighting qualities equal to other game fish of the same poundage. Perhaps last summer I had more occasion to notice this in southwestern New Brunswick than elsewhere. I was using a very light casting rod of the sort which might very correctly be called the tournament type—the kind made for the lightest lures. Nevertheless, I used all models of universal bass baits of wood, metal and feathers. The pickerel in the neighborhood fought harder than the brook trout I caught in the streams near by and leaped out of water as agilely and as frequently as small-mouth bass.

You will find pickerel close to logs, in bogs, moss beds, lily pads, muskeg or heather or weeds in shallow water with a sandy, soft bottom that small-mouths avoid, though now and then you see them close together in deeper and rocky stream water. Pickerel respond well to surface and semi-underwater lures, and those which are equipped with weed guards come in mighty handy because these fish seem to frequent places where these hook entanglements are very plentiful. The spinning and darting underwater lures, either with or without pork rind, seem also to have a way of taking their fancy.

When pickerel were in a striking mood, I have, in a single day, just for the sake of experiment, tried out twenty-five different kinds of lures and caught as many on one as on another. If they had a favorite, it was a grooved-head, red and white plug. No special maneuvering of the plug was necessary—fast or slow and sometimes at rest —it had equal claims. One of the most skilled pickerel casters with whom I ever fished usually dropped his lure on a lily pad, rock or log, then jerked it off, like a frog jumping in the water. I have a few times seen a pickerel, hooked and then lost in the moss, come back for the same lure which was tormenting it a moment before.

The wall-eyed pike which, in so many parts of the North, is called "pickerel" or doré is not a pickerel nor a member of the family Esocidæ, but a pike-perch, with prominent dorsal fins of the fresh water perch tribe. It is regarded as one of the most excellent table fish found on the North American continent. Its habitat is even more extensive in the North than that of the bass and it is another game fish which strikes at almost any of the artificial lures, though usually it does not put up the spectacular resistance of many other game varieties. Sometimes they attain pretty good weight; as evidence, we cite the instance of a catch in Current River, in Missouri, of one weighing sixteen and one-half pounds.

CASTING FOR MUSKIES AND PIKE

In many streams and lakes wall-eyed pike are caught on hard, sandy or rocky bottoms with all types of casting lures. The semi-underwater and underwater lures are best. Wall-eyes do not come well to surface baits. They are not quick strikers, but move slowly, so that the man who reels indolently in the proper places gets the most fish. Often they like to wait for prey in fairly deep water at the subsidence of a fall or rapid.

At Pine Camp Rapids, French River, Ontario, one time I had numerous strikes from wall-eyes while using a Silver Doctor weighted casting feather minnow with a pork rind attached. They were seemingly most attracted by the strip of pork and bit at it, thus avoiding being caught on the hook. After a time, realizing this, I used only half of the usual length of strip and managed to hook two-thirds of my strikes.

Once an angler connects with a muskellunge while using light bait-casting tackle, he experiences a never-to-be-forgotten thrill. For awhile, he is willing to believe he is hooked on to a wild bull with amazing strength, resourcefulness, and fighting versatility past crediting. The strength of these long, bull-terrier-muzzled, wickedly armed creatures is something to consider; and only when you take this under advisement will you have much success in landing them with the sort of bait-casting tackle you use for bass. It is excusable to use stiff, heavy rods and heavy test lines when you decide to use large, heavy lures.

Strange to say, many of the largest muskies ever caught while casting were attracted by small-size lures. But, anglers are prone to use the large ones because the hooks are large and the lures are more likely to remain intact after the first wicked smash. Many fishermen who catch big muskies persist, however, in using small lures and fine lines, proceeding under the theory that the lighter the tackle with which they are landed the more thrilling the engagement.

There are two wooden lures which are my personal favorites—and I never use larger than the five-eighths-ounce bass size. One is the standard red and white plug, from which design so many other varieties are made, and the other, which never travels below the surface, is of light wood with metal spinners at each end. But personal piscatorial loves must not be regarded as the only ones worth trying. On the contrary, muskies will attack any bucktail or large feathered spoon and darting or wobbling bait. Those which will not attract this vicious member of the pike family are usually ones that never see action outside of a tackle kit!

Many anglers take keen delight in discovering the resorting places of muskies in lakes and streams, while others depend on local guides and thus save time by avoiding useless casting territory. Unless you know a large lake, you are bound to miss certain shoals, reefs and weed beds that are musky infested, though they are known to every man and child in the neighborhood.

The best times of the year for casting for muskies are early in the summer and early and late in the fall. From this, however, the angler is not to imagine that none whatever are taken in midsummer. At that period some respond, but not nearly so avidly as earlier and later. The fall musky is really a more resourceful and wicked fighter. The theory that all, or at least part, of them suffer from dentition troubles in summer has listed at least myself as a convert. On several occasions this season I personally examined muskies of various sizes having sore gums. Some had loose teeth that I easily pulled out with my fingers and some had shed their teeth and the new arrivals in their place were already in evidence.

As with big northern pike, always use a bronze cable or piano wire leader connecting your line with your lure. Personally, I prefer the bronze cable wire. It is not so likely to give the lure an impotent action from getting a sudden kink in it. Work the best looking places and go by no weed bed, rocky or log-strewn pocket without making several casts.

The instant a musky strikes, be prepared for war. Frequently, the big boy starts with a leap from the water and, failing to eject the lure, apparently reels in submissively to your boat. Then do not be deceived, but be on your guard immediately. Though you are ever so eager to land that fish, be ready to give slack instantly, for at this crucial moment most of the tigerish finny warriors are lost. The tyro, feeling that he has conquered his quarry by its apparent docile behavior, begins reeling fast and hard, endeavoring to bring the fish closer to the boat. All at once, Mr. Musky wakes up. The sudden taut line is the opportunity for which he has been waiting. Unexpectedly the water begins to seethe in circles where you had the musky a moment previously. Then you feel slack. The big fish has broken the line with ease and is swimming to some aqueous crypt, free and in possession of one of your favorite baits.

When you hook a big musky, play him with intelligence and skill. Let it be a battle of give and take, yielding line when you find the battle too strenuous and recovering when slack is accorded. There will be several regal leaps, vicious dashes and the deceptive lulls when you may think the fish is worn and quitting, but he is only recovering strength and mental poise for another desperate rush, standing, tail on end, and scurrying around in that position in a half circle.

I never trust a big musky till I actually feel that it has had all the fight taken out of it. Twice I have seen one leap clear across a canoe and put myself and my line in a hazardous position just when my companion was offering him a position in a landing net. Wait for astounding virility at the last moment, and only when you are certain that the end is near be tempted to perform the final coup de grace.

I like a big landing net or gaff. Shooting a musky has always appeared to me unsportsmanlike, if it is done before the fish is entirely conquered and brought close to the boat.

My mind sways between classifying pike as real

fighters or noncombatants. It is because the characteristics of these fish vary so much. I have caught hundreds of them that were rank quitters and then the very opposite prevailed, some of the big boys performing as desperately as the wickedest musky I ever hooked. In the North Country this occurs regularly, because it is very difficult to find a lake where northern pike are not plentiful and you will connect with many quitters before you hang on to one that is a strong, lasting fighter. The Ojibwas of the famed Nipigon country will bear me out in my statement when I declare that I have seen them as large in size as any musky existing and weighing, doubtless, between fifty and sixty pounds. In fact, I watched one in Lake Polly, a back spread of the Nipigon, tow a languid angler around in a canoe for an hour before he finally parted company with him.

Such occasions as this one I note are the reasons for my debating with myself as to their gameness. I have struck a big one around thirty pounds without getting much display of belligerence; then another leaped, dashed and cut up in every way before I stopped him. Once, while floating down French River a few miles above the French River camp I hung to an enormous pike. He ran for a little bay, then quit immediately. Ten minutes later close to camp I hooked one that weighed, at the most, not over six pounds. But he certainly fought—fast and furiously—and no fish of his poundage ever gave me a more forceful or longer battle.

Wire leaders are necessary when casting for pike. They have an abiding penchant for cutting lines not so equipped. Almost any casting bait, when the fish are in the mood, will bring a response. Do not reel too fast, for though they have speed they strike to kill their prey and often miss being hooked when the lure travels too swiftly. In some waters, if they see you it matters little. If the lure attracts them, they will smash it just the same. When hungry or angry, they are desperate. At Lake Helen, the last big spread of the Nipigon, while in the company of two Ojibwas, Dan Moriseau and Harry Le Sage, I hit into a fair-sized pike. Immediately, he cut my line and I saw him boring deep with my yellow and red plug fastened to his jaw. Whereat, I quickly attached another plug of a green-scale finish to my line and cast it where the pike had disappeared behind a rock. To my amazement, he came for the second lure, seized it and shortly

133

after I landed him and recovered my first lure, which was still rigidly fastened in his mouth.

But in sections not so remote from the daily infestations of hordes of anglers, northern pike become wary and are just as shy of making human acquaintances as bass. They are fond of attacking all artificial lures, and with a light whippy bait-casting rod often put up a long, formidable combat. In the lower Nipigon, where it brawls into that long, tumultuous race en route to pour its flow into the clear blue of Lake Superior, while casting for the immense trout which are found there I have struck small pike in the rapids and been unable to distinguish whether it was a huge brook trout or a pike—so similar was their battling—until I coaxed it into calm, transparent water.

Pike fishing is typically a bait caster's sport. Pike are abundant in so many places that they fill in empty angling hours when bass and other game fish are not on the rise.

CHAPTER XIII

TACKLE KITS AND ACCESSORIES

THE value of a good tackle kit proves its worth in bait casting wherever fishing exists and from the first day it is put in service. We are all guided by our financial means and the amount of tackle we like or care to take along on our fishing trips. Nothing can compare with a good one for compactness and convenience, and, best of all, they are manufactured for every size purse and desire. Trying to carry casting lures in a bag or pocket brings nothing but trouble. If the hooks are not catching and entangling in each other, they snag the clothes and nothing can be found the instant you want it, only a formidable disarray of angling requisites that often cause the owner untold labor to disengage them piece by piece.

Each tackle kit should have separate compartments for lures, lines, reels and other necessities. Those of heavy metal that will keep their shape should be selected. If they are a little heavy, they protect your outfit so much the better. The trays will invariably be found to fit the designated places. Some are made *de luxe* with leather covers, but this is not absolutely necessary, though water-shedding qualities are. No tackle kit should be too high; the limit of height ought to conform to the room under the seat of a rowboat and preference should be given to length instead of weight. Just visualize a box arrangement for containing tackle that adapts itself to easy storage in a boat, canoe or at home, and you will arrive at the right idea of the style of tackle box which will most please you. But above all guard against easily dented affairs of thin metal. They are practical for a short trip and that is about the limit of their duration. You know the waters you fish, how much you want to take along, so let it regulate your tackle kit predilections.

If you go in for light, cheap affairs, confine them to small ones, such as are suitable for a day's wading, which contain but a limited supply and fit in one of the pockets of your fishing coat. You can, with a little perfunctory observation, find in any tackle store the kit most adaptable to your fishing and means of travel.

Take care of the kit. Several times during

your fishing trip, and just before you store your things away during the idle season, empty it of all its contents, wipe them, and the kit clean, and then expose it to the sun until you are sure no moisture remains in it. This is not much trouble and inevitably pays returns in leaving your tackle always in tip-top shape.

When the writer begins to think of a list of accessories, there are two which always come at the top: a pair of pliers and a can of oil, the kind which is found in tackle stores, having a top guaranteed absolutely against leakage. The oil is necessary every day for reels. The pliers will come in handy in almost every imaginable way, especially when you get a hook in your hand or some other precious part of your anatomy. Use them then to cut the eyed part of the hook. Then push the hook through past the barb and pull it out with the pliers, thereby saving further worry and pain.

A box of waterproof matches for wet days in case of rain or an unexpected immersion is worth considering; also a small bottle of iodine so you can immediately sterilize any abrasion, cut or wound. A little piece of cloth for rubbing things might well come within the category of first things to be considered among fishing accessories. Also, some adhesive tape for dressing wounds and mending things. Now add to your kit connecting links, swivels, snap and weighted, and above all cable or piano wire leaders. Connecting links save much work while changing lures. If you do not use cable or piano wire leaders, prepare to lose many lures when pike or musky fishing. These sharp-toothed warriors have a marvelous habit of cutting expensive silk lines.

Every sort of casting weight will come in handy when least expected. Get a supply of different sizes from the regular dipsey kinds to those weighted with snaps. This will help in your scheme of casting extremely light lures or making your ordinary ones travel deeper than their wont. Do not be satisfied with a single variety. Instead, pin your faith to a good assortment for all purposes.

Fish stringers are important, especially those of cord with the efficient stringing needle. Bass will live for ages on them and keep fresh if you string them by running the stringer through the upper and lower part of the mouth. Doing this *via* the gills is only a quick way of killing them. A fish scaler and knife for all purposes should be

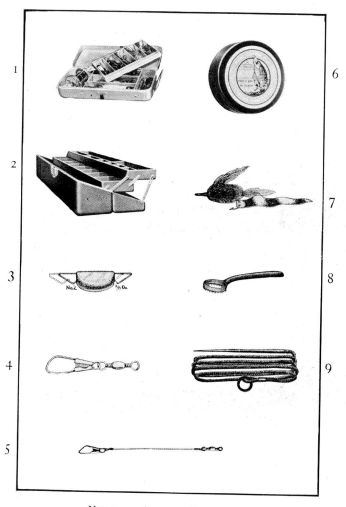

NECESSARY ANGLING ACCESSORIES

1. Pocket tackle kit
2. Standard tackle kit
3. Casting sinker
4. Snap swivel sinker
5. Piano wire leader

6. Braided silk bait casting line
7. Pork rind strip
8. Fish scaler
9. Fish stringer

companions of the stringer, and you never know how much service a disgorger really gives until you are after a hook which has become deep imbedded in the mouth of a pike or musky. All these aids take up little room and more than repay the thought of providing them when their use is required daily.

Then remember wrapping silk, a candle, ferrule cement, and just a wee bit of the coil solder that comes in such nice form for neophytes. Wrapping silk, especially if you have a small bottle of varnish, a candle, and ferrule cement are invaluable first aids when you have rod troubles, and solder helps with steel rods. I never go on a fishing trip without providing myself with a few extra screws for my reels and at least one extra handle for my favorite, lest an accident happen to put it out of commission. A small bit of fine copper wire wrapped in compact shape will store nicely in a tackle box and be welcomed on many occasions.

I consider all the things mentioned above as absolutely necessary, and one more which ought not be overlooked, though included last, is a few additional male and female ferrules for bamboo rods. Be sure they are the right size. They are as indispensable as a small pair of scissors, for they are about the hardest things, of an angler's equipment, to find in a country store.

Folding landing nets and gaffs fit some tackle kits, but not all. Nevertheless, they ought not to be neglected. Though you may safely land bass with your hands, beware of doing it with musky, pickerel, pike and even the harmless-looking wall-eyes. Those wicked, menacing teeth are not to be disregarded. Many shoot an apparently conquered muskellunge, but to me it has always been an unsportsmanlike method of terminating the engagement of a real fighting fish, for he still has a chance to fight while being netted or gaffed. The wall-eyed pike does not frighten much with his harmless dental arrangement. Watch out, however, for his gill covers. There is a little round sharp part on them with which they inflict a nasty wound when not handled with this possibility in mind.

Extra hooks, regular models and weedless ones, are always required. For plugs, there is an ingeniously made lot which can be attached to the eye of every lure by merely slipping them on or off. They are of exceedingly good quality. No angler ought ever to overlook an extra lot of bucktails, feathered and hair flies of the regular and weedless varieties. They can be quickly substituted for one that is lost or broken without delaying the fishing.

The best bait casters are often those who stress accuracy and consistently keep working the likely spots of the fishing ground; yet with all the skill at their command and mastery of fish knowledge, if they are not supplied with the necessary accessories, most of their sport is marred when something goes wrong with the outfit.

CHAPTER XIV

REPAIRING RODS AND CARING FOR FLIES

THE angler who is persistent with bamboo or wooden fly- and bait-casting rods finds at times that the matter of knowing how to repair them when anything goes wrong is of great interest to him. When breaks occur in the wilderness the first thing the average man thinks about is how in the world is he going to remedy matters? At home, too, the best fishing rods do not always escape trouble; they may be injured by some thoughtless member of the family storing them where they are apt to be broken, and handling by those unfamiliar with rods often places them out of commission when least anticipated. Personally I have fished with bait- and fly-casting rods for over thirty years and never had the misfortune to break one, but during this period it has been a pleasure to help many anglers make quick repairs so they could return to their fishing with very little intermission.

I think the majority of anglers have experience

with the effects that steam or other heat has on their rods. It dries out the varnish to the point of cracking and soon the windings are seen to fray and become unwrapped, though no human hand touched them. The varnish alone where it does not cover windings suffers a great deal until the angler sees that these matters must be remedied if he expects to fish with his favorites the following season.

Another ailment of bamboo fishing rods must be treated during the lulls between fishing season. You must take out the sets due to handling too heavy lures and spinners. Sometimes a vast amount of casting and constant fishing causes them to show up. And there are lots of other factors that enter into the existence of a rod which will develop these unsightly handicaps. A careful angler can take them out and restore the rod to its erstwhile straightness, but he must exercise caution lest he create more serious trouble than the one of the set. Bamboo is a material of nearly the same properties as horn in so far as it is affected by heat; a moderate application of heat makes it pliable, but too much heat will disintegrate the gluing of the rod. These repairs had best be left to an experienced rod maker who is expert in this line of work.

Heat the part very slowly where the set shows over a gas flame, holding it some distance from the flame so direct heat will not touch it. The warmth at a distance will gradually have its effect, and slowly you can bring back the section to the form it was in when it arrived from the factory. This work requires some time. Never try to hurry it, be satisfied to straighten it a little at a time until completion and then you will be assured that the gluing has not been injured.

This brings to mind the fact that often rods are declared to be made of exceedingly soft bamboo because they take a set very easily, yet the very opposite is the case. Possibly they are made of extremely hard Tonkin cane, but unknowingly have been subject to heat. The glue melted and came away from the strips and dried out in that condition. Nothing is left to hold the strips together except the silk wrappings, ferrules and varnish and this causes the angler incorrectly to attribute all its lack of casting power to the bamboo.

At the least sign of wrappings becoming frayed the rod should be entirely rewound. If the wrappings display no injury or defects, every year the rod ought to be varnished. This treatment will prevent wrappings from fraying, if nothing else, as well as improve the looks of the rod. Remove all the old varnish with fine steel wool, a piece of glass, or the very finest grained emery paper made. Do it slowly, but get off all the old varnish at all hazards. Do not touch the wrappings, however, if you wish to retain them.

The commercial rod varnishes are excellent, but if for the moment they are unobtainable you will get excellent results from standard quality spar varnish. There is no need to apply first a coat of shellac as some do. Start with the spar varnish, applying it thinly with a light fine camel's-hair brush, and avoiding any blistering by over-lavish treatment. Some get better results by putting the varnish on with their fingers and rubbing the rod lengthwise with a very meager application. This method guards perfectly against blisters. Put the rod where it will neither be touched by human hands nor gather dust. Be sure not to overlook the fact that a warm room causes the varnish to flow freely and dry slowly.

In recent years celluloid varnishes, most of them made by dissolving common celluloid in acetone, have been quite popular for rods. They will cause trouble if all old varnish has not been removed. Otherwise they are good and are advocated by experienced rod repairers.

Anglers differ as to the number of coats of varnish which should be applied to a rod. Without indulging in useless controversy we suggest that two are sufficient if they are applied properly, the second after the other has dried completely. Putting on too many coats often produces a beautiful finish, but when it starts to crack it comes off in large pieces, and it is not much effort to cause it to crack. Experts are able to put on three to six coats without a rod being thus afflicted; but those who do can never be graded in the matter as other than experts of much higher caliber than most anglers have ever occasion to become.

If the rod is to be finished entirely there is a bit of work ahead for the amateur operator, but it is much cheaper to have a rod rewound and revarnished, considering everything, than to do it yourself. If you wish to do it, go ahead, and take pleasure in doing it, or appreciate the setbacks you are sure to have at your initial attempt.

Provide yourself with winding silk. If you have trouble, particularly with fly rods and small bait-casting rod guides, holding the snake and other small guides in hand while you wrap a section, then stick them on with shellac. This will facilitate the matter.

Learn to tie the invisible knot by holding in readiness a small loop of wrapping silk in your left hand. Wind your last three or four, five or six times around it, leaving the end of the loop sufficiently beyond the last, so that you can thread into it the end. Then, grasping hold of the termination of the loop which you have not covered, draw it quickly under the last windings. This will hold as well as conceal the thread. But the start is made by laying the line toward your right almost as far as you intend to wrap, then start wrapping over it and continue. It will hide the straight thread and help in the matter of holding your winding.

Ferrule cement is the best thing to hold on your ferrules. So many nowadays much prefer the possibility of ferrules occasionally becoming loose, and use only regular ferrule cement to hold them, instead of having additionally a dowel, which, while it helps hold the ferrule on more securely, is thought to injure the integrity of the rod.

147

Breaks are repaired in the field by using a small flat file on each part and dressing it down for sufficient length to make an effective wrap after a very slight amount of ferrule cement or quick-drying glue has been applied. It is no great trouble to carry in the field a light repair outfit. Nothing in angling is so appreciated as a tiny serviceable outfit at your hands when your best rod happens to be broken or other injuries occur.

What appears in the closing part of this chapter will be found valuable to both bait and fly casters. It is just a hint on taking care of flies during the winter period, for the best and most attractive place for the dreaded moths to work is in the folds of a fly book. I know anglers who every year treat the bodies of their flies with a transparent celluloid preparation to protect them against the invasion of moths, and then apply all over their fly books camphor or other efficient moth preventives. Once in a while you see an angler who loves his flies so well that he places them after the fishing season is over in a mason jar, and then pours in a small amount of carbon bisulphide. He is not troubled with the invasions of any predatory insects, nor is the man who does the same things and sprinkles the flies with cedar oil or powdered camphor or puts in the container a generous supply of moth balls and then screws on the top firmly.

PART II
FLY CASTING

CHAPTER I

FLY CASTING

WHILE bait casting in its present stage can be justly considered as having enlisted in its ranks more participants in recent years than any other sort of angling, perhaps with the exception of those who use the humble worm or live bait, in no manner has it detracted from the fly-rod sport, nor even recruited many from the devotees of this wonderful pastime. However much they can see the merits of flinging artificial affairs in the lurking places of the gamy water denizens, they still hold the mastery of the longer and whippier rod in the same esteem they always did. Such is the tribute for both sports that each enlists annually new followers, yet never entirely eliminates one from the other sports.

The statements of the foregoing paragraph may be verified by days of visiting many of the noted fishing waters. There are more bait casters than ever before; the same can be said of fly fishers. The splendid sportsmanship of it all obtains when you hear sportsmen praise both of these methods of fishing, though some of them have personal experience only with one of them. The ambition of all fishermen, doubtless, is the taking of fish according to their tenets, and this is what both artificial bait and fly casters include in the pertinent sentence that they appreciate the quality of the sport provided more than the number of fish caught.

Neither tradition nor sentiment connected with bait casting can take away the privilege of saying that the number of fly fishermen is on the increase almost everywhere. Naturally, the automobile and the little motors attached to watercraft have brought the fishing outdoors nearer home. Railways have proclaimed piscatorial attractions along their routes so well that many who never fished before suddenly found they wanted to fish at the same place and with the same tools as have those whom they beheld in the amazingly attractive literature. Trout, bass, salmon and other game fish furnished such transcending sport to others; why should not they, too, indulge in it when it was so easy to reach during their summer vacation periods?

Fly fishing for trout for years had been a fishing pastime above the ordinary, a rhythm of poetical motion. Angling artistry and knowledge of the inhabitants of tinkling brooks; and sparkling, fast, coursing, wild waters, were praised in song and made all the more marvelous by actual indulgence. Moreover, to the neophyte or the casual observer, it had mystery attached to it and many fully believed the erroneous idea that only those who were particularly blessed could ever learn to cast a fly with any degree of proficiency.

For many years anglers admitted that salmon and trout of all varieties were the dominating urge of fly casters. If they could cast for these fish every year and occasionally land one of important poundage, or even a small number of little ones, they regarded an actual heaven as only something religiously connected with their favorite outdoor pastime, and the fish alone did not surpass all other thrills they had experienced. The possession of one or more fly books replete with every pattern and size of fly designed for taking game fish, together with a familiarity with each, when it ought to be used, also agreed with their conception about what a blissful hereafter should hold for them. These were their bibles, their bibles of angling records, their treasures of piscatorial information.

I believe to-day that were trout anglers to confess truthfully to some of their greatest thrills, chief among them would be the possession of an abundant assortment of flies in all sizes and patterns, and fancying how well they reproduced the things of nature—which a lot of them don't—and trying out new creations of exquisitely designed millinery which they believe feasible, though no one has ever tried them before in the waters they whip.

You may argue for hours that, if in mood, trout will very frequently strike out of sheer curiosity, for food, tiny feathered affairs of strange and varied coloration, when they will not rise to anything resembling a product of nature; and, yet, absolute conviction will not be forthcoming, although you have personally proved this theory innumerable times.

I recall a day last summer when I was just below the upper falls on the Jackfish River, Ontario. I took four fine trout on a Cahill, then lost the fly through a negligent back cast into a spruce behind me. My fishing companion lamented this because it happened to be the only one in my pos-

SPECIAL BASS AND TROUT FLIES

session. Nevertheless, I was obdurate in tying on a fly which nothing of nature ever hoped to resemble—a bass fly on No. 1/0 Model Perfect hook with a brown bucktail hackle, red body and two long yellow streamers.

Were those fish faithful to the No. 12 Cahill dry fly, to which they had been responding so nicely? Not a bit of it. Three big ones over two pounds responded, and many little ones that, at first, belied the possibility of ever being connected with a No. 1/0 hook.

A similar thing occurred in that beautiful trout stream, whose name escapes me now, running through the town of Woodstock, New Brunswick. My wife and I were advised to fish up the river some ten miles from the town. The stream was low. I waded across and whipped the pool opposite me with every trout fly I had of the supposed true-to-nature type. Thinking the fish were extremely cautious in that clear water, I shot fully sixty feet of line, alternating with wet and dry flies. After a time of unrewarded persistence, I concluded that no trout were there. Then into the picture along the opposite bend, her shadow indicating her presence, came my wife. Using but a short bit of line, she dropped into the water a

Jenny Lind bass fly—does nature produce anything like it? Immediately the water boiled and soon she had hooked on to the red and blue a nice, red-spotted trout from the very pool where all my offerings had been eschewed.

A great addition to the number of fly casters came from bass fishermen; bait casters and still fishermen became fly casters for bass, though it was mighty hard for the die-hard class ever to acknowledge that there was quite as much sport catching bass with flies as there was their beloved trout, or even to credit the Micropterus family with being as gamy fighters. First, it was with difficulty that they were induced to attempt fly fishing for bass on a modest scale. But after they did they began to discover these fish were rugged, formidable fighters, and quite frequently, under some conditions, they excelled the most beautiful fontinalis or leaping rainbow.

What brought most conviction among trout fishermen was the way the bass struck surface flies. When they saw them actually catapult their entire bronze anatomy at their supposed victim, then tear for freedom, and follow with their vigorous, cupping leap, they were convinced that there was more to fly fishing for bass than they had ever believed possible.

Fly fishing for bass came into favor with leaps and bounds. First, perhaps, the bass angler was a bait or fly caster. He started skittering, as the art is correctly termed, though then he believed he was strictly a fly fisherman, using a small spinner to which was connected a small bucktail or standard feathered fly. Often the line was tied directly to the spinner, though most used a leader just as in regular fly fishing. The sport he had instilled a desire to become a purist. Whereat ordinary bass flies were fished successfully, and quickly a decision followed to try the famous bass bugs, about which so much had been written.

Once he saw a bass smash an artificial cork-bodied bass bug, he discovered that it struck a fly harder than any other game fish, and that casting a bass bug properly required far more skill and power in casting than any wet or dry fly fishing he had ever done.

I might add, too, that casting with bass bugs taught more anglers in a short time the value of high class split bamboo rods with plenty of casting punch than trout fishing for years had done. As evidence, we present the fact that the new crop of fly casters usually possess the most powerful bamboo rods made for their weight, and, on the other hand, thousands and thousands of trout fishermen are found still casting with "weeping willow" affairs that really handicap their casting instead of improving it.

Fly fishing for bass and trout differs from no other sport in that it requires perfect tools to get the most out of it. And the one thing that can always be said of the high-class outfit is that it pays for itself in a short time by its durability and the additional pleasure it provides.

One who has ever fished purist fashion with flies will consider it the balance of his life the greatest sport. No other outdoor pastime, unless it be the hunting of game, compares with fly fishing. Its chief quality for claiming this exalted and merited position is that it is a pastime for all ages. Men who have passed their prime continue to indulge with the same zest as in their boyhood days. The fascinations cannot be overlooked; as an old fly caster said, "You have more combined opportunities in this sport than in any other and the only fault with it is that when you are whipping a stream no day is long enough—hours pass with the rapidity of minutes. You are always busy seeking likely places, studying insects and trying to discover flies which will bring the epochal bass or trout of your dreams."

A trained eye becomes a requisite, for the urge of accuracy is as important to a fly caster as it is to the hunter. He delights in his proficiency; most of all on account of being near real, mist-laden water, in the real outdoors; he realizes the loftiest charms of nature in the stillness of the isolated region where he expects to encounter the biggest thrill of his existence close to a log or rock or the very next bend on the singing water-way.

There are fly fishermen galore and each ad-mits that one of the most engaging features of his sport is that with the right rod he can derive almost as much pleasure from hooking a small fish as a big one. And there is another thing which they never forget: the happy days success-fully casting the right fly, for this feature of their sport they have always with them.

CHAPTER II

FLY-ROD FACTS

QUITE frequently excellent writers on angling overlook an important factor when they dwell so informatively on the subject of fly-fishing rods, and that is the matter of price. One man can afford to pay any amount of money for one of the *de luxe* affairs, and another is limited to the expenditure of only a few dollars. The suggestions in this chapter will bear this in mind, though they will not forget that attention must be directed to casting power and durability of fly rods even when the matter of cost is important. Another matter worthy of note is that, no matter what the personal opinions and predilections of the writer may be, he cannot avoid the fact that one type of rod may suit one man and may yet be altogether unsatisfactory to another.

With the advancement of the use of steel fishing rods, there came on the market fly rods made of steel. Quite contrary to the claims of the users of steel fly rods, at no time did the makers of these articles boast that such products compared with the best made of bamboo. Their just contention—which seems well carried out—is that steel rods are only a substitute for bamboo and at no time do they possess the great casting power of that material, but they do have certain meritorious qualities and a fair steel rod can be purchased at a much lower price.

There are many times when a steel rod should take the place of a fine bamboo rod, particularly when an irresponsible friend wants to borrow a rod, also, if you and your friends are inveterate users of spinners. Constant use of spinners will inexorably put a bad set in a fine bamboo rod, but will not bother one of steel. When you or any other angler vary your fly-rod program with still fishing or trolling nothing will serve so well nor last so long as the modern steel affair.

If the steel rod for fly fishing has approximated the bamboo in any respect, it has been only in the light trout rods. There are some dainty little creations in this line which beginners will appreciate. The wrapping all over of steel rods with silk has increased their fishing value none, but may have helped their durability a great deal. The average fly rod made of steel in lengths ranging from nine to ten feet is absolutely too heavy and unwieldy. Some have the fault of being entirely too slow, reminding one of the erstwhile popular greenheart and lancewood products. On the other hand, many have a nasty kick-back or are afflicted with too much vibration at every movement. A good deal of the latter can be obliterated by using a heavier line than usual. Such a change often gives really a pleasant action.

In behalf of the average steel rod, it can be truthfully said that there are no silk wrappings to fray. They will stand much abuse and are fairly good for the fellow who cares nothing about a rod except when he is fishing.

We might say that fly rods of Bethabara, lancewood, and other such materials are fairly obsolete as far as universal use is concerned, although a few are still seen on the market or in the hands of unconvertible old-timers. They served well in their heyday of fishing activities. But, when bamboo got in the hands of anglers, the death knell of the old type of wooden rod was sounded. Besides their other obvious faults, they were altogether too slow and even the best of them could never pick up, with ease, the amount of line a rod properly manufactured of split bamboo could. Furthermore, their casting powers were deficient. Nevertheless, we have no quarrel to pick with those who still love the slow, weepy action. This they like; so why criticize adversely the material from which the tools are made which give them so much pleasure?

Many traditions have to be shattered when describing the manufacture of bamboo rods or other important matters connected with them. One of these is that a perfect rod must be handmade throughout. In our boyhood, we believed that, unless a bamboo rod were split by hand, it would suffer serious internal or other troubles; which, translated, means that the material was considered weakened when any machinery at all was used. Old-timers told, seriously, that machinery invariably weakened the enamel and the enamel was the secret of the strength of a rod.

Bamboo split by machinery shows greater exactness than the hand work. Furthermore, the strength of the bamboo is not in the enamel but in the hard fiber between the pith and the enamel, though, doubtless, the strength of the enamel alone adds a little, as well, to the finish and other kindred requisites.

A number of years ago, when the Cross Rod

165

plant was at Lynn, Massachusetts, I had many occasions to visit it, being on terms of close acquaintance with its managers and corps of rod makers. Mr. Forsythe, now deceased, had a hobby for experimenting with bamboo, in every stage of its growth, the so-called different varieties, and especially the difference effected by hand work and machinery. Many times I saw him split by hand, then split by machinery, and then test for the difference in tensile strength Every time the machine work showed best, especially in that most important matter of gluing.

An irrefutable bit of information is associated with some of the various highly touted rods made by anglers for themselves or by certain makers who cater to the public as producers of the real, handmade articles. Nevertheless, a number of these are selected, split and glued by machinery at some of the well-known rod plants. These sticks, as they are then called, are bought by the putative handmade rod makers, and all they do throughout the process of preparing them for the market is to mount them, wrap and varnish them. In some instances, even the mountings are made at the factories, though in descriptive literature they are termed as being of their own handmade fabrication. But, in connection with these rods, I have to state that, despite their somewhat dubious authenticity, they are the equals of any fly rods made, whether of foreign or American origin.

It is impossible to deny several things linked closely with rod making, production cost and selling cost; the profits in rod making, considering the necessary advertising, the vagaries of marketing channels and the extra disbursements each ramification requires, are exceedingly small. Cheap rods have to have big distribution before they will return profits to the makers. Expensive rods are more susceptible to elasticity in prices, because not so many are sold competitively. Profits with them are not estimated on the big production basis, but through a fair return on each, as though they were made and sold in a leisurely fashion, which comes pretty near being the truth.

A high-class split bamboo rod goes through a certain manufacturing itinerary with slight variations. We will spare readers the arguments as to the relative merits of Calcutta and Tonkin-bamboo for fly rods. After all, it simmers down to the action favored. Several noted rod makers who have spent almost a lifetime experimenting

167

with split bamboo allege that, for hard action necessary for dry fly fishing and casting the large modern fly rod lures for bass, the dirty-sided sticks are best. They explain that bamboo is of a quick growth. The dirty side butt pieces are the ones which face the prevailing wind of the country, and therefore, are much tougher than any other part. These sticks go into high-class rods.

The sticks are first seasoned. This requires in a dry temperature at least six months after the bamboo has arrived. They are then split by machinery and glued. Afterward, they are wrapped with twine and left six months more to cure as glued sticks. However well they may be dressed, if the split sticks are not cured again before being glued the rod later is affected. During the curing after they are split, the split sides swell a little or bulge in parts, but, when entirely cured, this disappears. Naturally, rods made on a big production basis must miss a good many of these vitals to rod making, all of which cost money; and that is the reason that they often spread apart and become unshapely, also, they do not require the extra expense of selection as high-grade rods. The cheap ones show assembly of the right sizes and parts for completing a rod

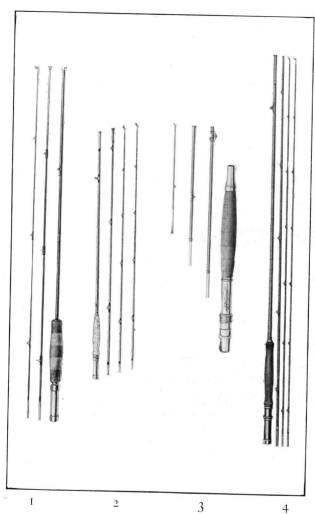

| I | 2 | 3 | 4 |

UNIVERSALLY USED TYPES OF FLY RODS

1. Jointed split bamboo fly rod
2. Three-ounce jointed split bamboo fly rod
3. Jointed steel fly rod
4. Jointed split bamboo dry fly rod

more than they show the choosing of each bit with the same grain in each joint and other matters about which few anglers ever think.

The winding, mounting and varnishing, to complete a rod, can cover many sins, through the insistence of some fishermen for a fly rod at an extremely low figure. And they get in full what they pay for.

Some of the very cheap rods made *via* the big production route have in them the very same bamboo used in the most expensive rods. I know personally one manufacturer who makes nothing but the most expensive rods who sells to an exceedingly large manufacturer of rods for jobbing houses all split sticks which have suffered from big slivers coming off them when run through the machinery. When assembled in a rod, these marrings of the surface often have no serious effect on the finished rod. In fact, not long ago I handled one which had marvelous power. It was a five and three-quarters ounce rod, retailing at eight dollars. This cheap affair picked up from ninety to one hundred feet of C to H English tournament fly line as well as any strictly built-for-the-purpose, high-grade rod of the same weight I have ever seen. I could see the surface defects, the groove made by a stripping sliver. I knew nothing about the seasoning or the gluing, but if that rod does not stand up for any length of time, so excellent is the material from which it is made, it will pay the owner to have it rebuilt properly.

Production basis rods show no limit to the character of the wrappings, mountings or styles of manufacture. The majority of them are marketed under a private label, so that the buyer never knows the maker, and some of the names under which they are sold are characteristic of American selling ingenuity.

In buying a high-grade rod, the writer feels the best advice that he can give is to purchase only the kind made by well-known manufacturers. Then, if the rod is faulty in any respect, he can take the matter up with the rod maker and be quickly provided with any repair part when needed. Most of them take personal pride in their products and are very willing immediately to remedy a fault for which they are responsible. Imperfect rods get out somehow, despite their exceeding alertness. Once in a while bamboo which looks perfect and acts perfect when first made up into a rod goes wrong. The maker is always ready to help the buyer out during any of these troubles and takes the blame for that one erratic product himself.

During the making of a high-class fly rod, the true craftsman endeavors to make the entire rod, so far as possible, from one butt piece. This has been praised by writers on the subject. But the use of separate pieces pans out nearly every time fully as well since the real artist is exceedingly careful in selecting, keeping the grain straight and even throughout, though he has to labor diligently day after day in deft heating and straightening to make a rod in the perfect lines he has in mind from butt to tip.

Even rods of the same caliber measurements, built the same throughout, will differ. I do not believe the most expert rod makers in the world will ever be able to avoid this; yet they are everlastingly striving for excellence of product and I perpetually marvel at how they can turn out six-strip split bamboo rods as cheaply as they do, considering the time, labor and materials involved in the making.

Tests of rods show that six-strip affairs are by far the best. More or less strips sacrifice an inexplicable something. To increase their strength, some rod makers have devious ways of attaining their end; some by having a thin steel core in the center, which is of no avail except to sacrifice casting power and add weight. Winding rods luxuriously every inch between joints only softens them a bit and detracts from casting power. Many of the greatest tournament distance casters prefer rods wrapped only at the ferrules and mountings. Among these actual and supposed aids to strength, the best I have seen are built of two layers of bamboo in each strip. The manufacturer has added strength and casting power, yet has kept the weight practically down to the standard of other rods.

In recent years there has been a trend on the part of bamboo rod makers to stain their rods in various shades of brown. It really gives them an attractive appearance and, possibly, does not reflect light so much as the natural finish. A few rod makers who are providing rods thus adorned stated that the preparation they use adds strength to the bamboo. The reputation which they have gained for integrity and performance through their rods leads one to believe that there must be something back of their statements.

Individual tastes differ so much that it is a difficult matter to say just what sort of rod each angler ought to have. Naturally, the best guides are the sort of fishing and the waters upon which it is done. If the purse permits, it is best to buy the highest class rods obtainable, though there are lots of medium-priced ones which give excellent service for long periods. The beginner will invariably declare that he is a dub at first, just learning, and what is the use of having a high-grade rod while he is still only a neophyte? Against this is offered the fact that he will learn more quickly with a good rod. If he gives it any attention, it will be good practically forever and outlast many cheap rods which will possibly not give satisfaction and will interfere considerably with his progress in casting. All he has to do to preserve it intact to hand it down to his grandchildren is to have it rewrapped and varnished every few years. If he starts with a cheap rod it will not be in existence very long.

As some fish only tiny brooks, very light rods of short length will serve them, even as light as two or two and one-half ounces, and only seven or seven and one-half feet long. Particularly if the fish run small will they enjoy whippiness in order to get all possible sport out of the tiniest trout, within the legal limit. Yet do not overlook the fact that some of these very light, short rods can have almost as hard an action as one of five or six ounces. The writer has one weighing two and one-half ounces, seven and one-half feet long which is so powerful it will shoot seventy-five feet of fly line with no great difficulty and it requires at least a D line to pull out its action for efficient casting. In a narrow stream it is impossible to cast well a tapered line with it, for a certain amount of line weight is necessary before it will have fishing proficiency.

A good deal can be written on selecting rods. Very few rods really show their innate powers until they have the proper fly line on them. For ordinary fly casting for trout and different varieties of small game fish an action which is slightly soft will not hurt. But for dry-fly casting as well as difficult bass bugs, hard action rods with lots of backbone are absolutely necessary for good work. The fly-rod lures, like bass bugs and feather minnows, encounter considerable air resistance and you have to have power in a rod in order to cast them at the proper distance. Dry-fly casting tests the vitality of a good rod in a short time. If the

174

rod has no backbone, it will fall down on its required work before very long.

Rods should not be estimated by their weight, as many light rods have greater casting ability than much heavier ones. Five and three-quarters to six ounces seems to be the ethical weight for fly fishing for bass. Under this weight, rods have most call from trout fishermen. The best advice that can be given to a beginner is to have his dealer help him to select a rod for his kind of fishing and see that the rod and the line balance. For, again, remember that rods of the same weight may differ in action and one that will handle a certain line will not handle another. As for lengths, visualize the streams you fish. If narrow or closely grown with brush, short fly rods under nine feet are mighty handy. Long ago we believed in lengths of ten feet and over for casting long distances in the open, but a nine and one-half foot rod will shoot as great a distance as an angler can strike a fish properly and promptly.

CHAPTER III

FLY LINES, LEADERS AND REELS

IN these days the beginner does not trust to his powers of discovery or an intuitive knowledge to lead him miraculously to select the proper equipment for his proposed angling pastime. He is willing to believe that certain mysteries remain veiled for neophytes in the fly-casting game but, on the other hand, a sportsman's credulity leads him to think that, if he learns what are the favorite tools of an expert, he has discovered inevitably the right road to becoming expert. He does not always aspire to the skill of the champions, but to the proper knowledge of how to take bass or trout.

Much praise must be accorded manufacturers of equipment for fly fishing if for no other reason than that they make very or fairly serviceable goods for anglers which, though they accommodate any size of purse, will be of some service in angling. This is a tribute which must be paid them, for, in plain words, they put the great sport of casting a fly within reach of all. This I am considering of the greatest importance in this chapter, though every once in a while you may think the description of certain products is a suggestion that you possess them as soon as possible. The man who lives above his means is a pitiable object, but he cannot be blamed for doing it when buying equipment while the urge is on and he wishes to excel the skill of some friend which is symbolized at every vacant space on the walls in a den and very often elsewhere by exceedingly large trout or bass.

For a couple of dollars or so a fly line can be purchased which will give really good service. Usually it is called oiled silk, which it often is not, because oil and pure silk do not agree with each other. Linen is substituted and is far better when the line is treated according to the oil method. These lines are strong and hard, and from an expert's standpoint too hard for distance or delicate casting. But if a beginner wishes he can start with them, learn fly casting properly and catch fish as well. All of the cheap lines are made level, that is to say, they are all of the same size throughout their length. They are adaptable to wet fly or bass-bug fishing, also, for skittering with spinners, but not for the best dry-fly casting, as they are not tapered. They should be kept out of the sun or any artificial heat. If not, the dressing will melt off them.

There is another grade of lines which is a little more expensive. These lines are usually made in the same colors as the most expensive American and English fly lines. While they, too, are serviceable for awhile their finish is likely to deceive a beginner who cannot see any difference between them and the vacuum-dressed lines with the soft finish. This is because they are treated with a celluloid enamel and have an exceedingly attractive appearance when coiled on a card and arranged for sale in a tastily designed container. Unfortunately, their finish cracks and with a little wear all that is used scales off completely.

There are some fairly high-grade lines manufactured with a celluloid finish, which are really of assistance to a beginner and scarcely affected much more by heat than more expensive kinds.

The best fly lines of the American and English manufacturers are finished by a process known as the vacuum process. Each maker has his own methods. American makers seemingly adhere to silk for their lines, while most of the best English products supposed to be silk are made of linen, which probably accounts for their strength and durability. Such high-grade lines undergo considerable manipulation. They are dressed and redressed, then cured for a time after each stage of treatment and finished with the secret process; some occasionally are made known which the fabricators have found to be best. These high-grade lines are made level, single or double tapered. The double-tapered ones obtain their value in the substantial fact that when one taper becomes used up, the other is available. The size of taper usually is the standard one of H, which greatly facilitates the casting, as well as delicately placing on the water, of small flies.

Quite a bit of controversy exists among exceedingly skilled anglers as to the right amount of taper a fly line should have. Tournament casters who contest in distance competition are very exacting. They want sufficient weight of line for casting, but they go in for taper to the extent very often of forty feet, the thickest part of the line being C until the thickness gradually comes down so that the last forty feet are size H. On account of the longer taper—which is excessive—such a line would be impractical for fishing. The main

179

idea is to have sufficient thickness to give line weight for the long cast, the taper partly to avoid air resistance and assist in the shoot for distance. If lines of such character were full length size C, it would be next to impossible to pick up a hundred feet or more with the rods now used, for the back cast, which is nothing more, when properly achieved, than the proper preparation for the forward cast.

Anglers starting the fly-fishing game need worry little about distance tournament casting or tournament lines. What would be best for them to observe most in the tournament sport is dry fly and not accuracy events. They will be of great value and interest to them.

Though tapered fly lines are used invariably by dry-fly casters in fishing, I know of some very efficient dry-fly casters who are exceedingly partial to a rod of a certain weight and always use level lines. Their reasons are easy for beginners to understand, particularly if they use one rod only for all purposes. The claim of the level dry-fly casters is often well borne out in experience. If they are using their pet dry-fly rod on a small narrow stream no wider than the taper, or the casting opportunity is no longer than the tapered part, the action is so hard that then there is not sufficient weight in a tapered line for them to cast it efficiently. This is the explanation of many dry-fly casters as to why they persist in using level lines.

In casting spinners, large flies, or cork-bodied fly-rod lures, like bass bugs, feather minnows and the present large bucktail and hair creations, a level line is in every particular the best. It will shoot the feathered deceits well. When using a tapered line with these flies, air resistance is encountered, the thinner part is very much inclined to belly and, however much you strive to prevent it, a part of the line will touch the water before your fly, especially if your cast is of considerable distance. This is one reason we find so many bass bugs and feather minnow casters who never use a leader over three or four feet in length or, at the most, five.

Fly lines require considerable attention. If it is given to them, they ought to last for years. They should be dressed regularly and taken off the reels after use. There are especially made large wooden reels for storing them. In case it is not feasible to use one, or they are too bulky to carry on a trip, take the line off the reel and hang it up somewhere in a hank until wanted. Keeping a fly line continually on a reel will cause it to crack eventually though it is the highest grade obtainable.

The favorite preparation for dressing fly lines is deer fat. Why this animal's fat is regarded as better than any other I have never been able to discover. Special preparations are on the market that surpass it in every way. Tournament casters, as well as many anglers, go to great pains to give their lines an additional dressing of graphite. Naturally this helps the shoot as it obviates practically all friction from the guides and tip top, but the line, after such a treatment, is messy and continually soiling the hands.

A fly rod should be examined frequently to see that all the guides are intact and have not become worn. The slightest rough surface will have an abrasive tendency and, if it does not cut the line, it will quickly strip off all the finish. Often I have seen anglers complain of the poor quality of the finish on their expensive lines, when all the trouble was finally traced to a defective guide.

There are leaders of all degrees of strength and quality. The novice need only ask his dealer for the best. He will be unable to detect quality.

Few anglers can, though they imagine they can, and they have to depend on the manufacturer's brand and the manufacturer on what the producers of silkworm gut abroad have to offer. The American manufacturer buys the silkworm gut in packages of strands and he ties them in the different lengths, according to thickness. Some are stained in light blue, green, brown, etc., to detract from their possible visibility in different waters, though the natural color, as a whole, in most streams is as invisible as needed. The stories of the tests for weight strain to which they are put to determine how much pulling they will stand are not the fiction of the American tackle jobbers but an actual fact. While stretching them to get them straight, with no kinks, lead weights are suspended from them and thus their powers are known. They average stronger than their alleged strength.

Some leaders are camouflaged to make them invisible to fish in different waters. A camouflaged leader shows several colors and aptly fills the bill in the dark waters of the North.

Japanese imitation gut leaders are big sellers on the American market because they are made knotless. They are artificially prepared, and are

183

quite inexpensive—their chief merit. The objection to them is principally that they become soft in a short time, but they can be tied right off to a hook without much preparatory contact with moisture or water, without breaking during the process.

Standard fly reels are all single action. The writer has never yet had occasion to discover why certain authorities on angling stress the point that a reel should balance a rod. All the try-outs on this subject have failed to bring out a single convincing argument in favor of certain reels for certain rods. In fact, by dispensing with a reel entirely, I have been able to cast as far as, if not farther, without a reel than with. Distance tournament casting of any consequence repeatedly demonstrates the same thing. Yet there are many old-timers who insist on heavy reels to balance, as they say, their rods. Some of the old school, noticeably Emerson Hough, would use a small lead coil for additional weight for balancing. All this seemed only a handicap of added weight.

A fly reel is merely a storage space for your fly line, keeping it out of trouble when necessary and adding a lot of sport while fighting a game fish. Yet some will still strip in a fish, despite having a reel, when they are losing half the pleasure, by so doing, that the trout or bass would otherwise have provided.

The handle on your fly reel should be small and narrow. All the best designs combine the two very important features: both handle and entire structure made so that they will always be out of the way of the line. The functioning should be simple, perfect, with a click so that the line will run out only when it is needed. There are both expensive and inexpensive varieties, both serving their purpose well. Uusually they are finished in dark gun metal, a sensible idea to prevent the reflecting of light that doubtless frightens wary fish. Select one that is not too heavy but will store a regular twenty-five, thirty, or thirty-three yard fly line, of size C or D, and an additional fifty yards of fine casting line, as a supplementary aid while fighting big fish in roomy fishing waters. There must be room for the thick heavy lines.

Some excellent reels are made of a material similar to pyralin. They are light, exceedingly strong and large enough to store a considerable amount of line. Reels with an agate guide help, as well as assist in maintaining the integrity of the enamel.

CHAPTER IV

THE ART OF FLY CASTING

POETRY of motion is the common description of fly casting and, whatever that may mean to the average man, to the angler it is an almost Biblical truth. The sweeping, graceful movement of the rod, the fly traveling through the air as though animated, then lightly descending on the water without disturbance, like a drowsing, spent insect, are verities, translated into sentimental form by anglers as the highest of arts associated with the blessings of the outdoors. We may have various emotions when witnessing or performing fly casting, but the least that can be said of them is that they endure; they are thrillingly ecstatic, and increase as expectancy urges every movement of the rod and drift of the fly.

The foregoing description of rods, lines, leaders and reels was to acquaint readers with the tools, in order that they might be in possession of serviceable ones when they began their first lessons in fly casting.

My preparatory advice is: instill confidence in yourself and make yourself believe that learning fly casting is very easy and that you will be able to master the fundamentals in fifteen minutes. The reason so many cast a fly poorly is that they never thought the fundamentals were worth learning, and went ahead right into fishing, continuing with the handicap of bad form and, worst of all, most of them refusing to admit it.

But it is always hard to get away from the universal idea that fly casting is difficult to master, and that it is an art only for those particularly gifted by nature. On the contrary, there is not one sport in existence so easy to learn. It requires very little intelligence, a fair wrist and arm, a good eye, and just a wee bit of patience. One may truthfully say that a delicate, skilled bait caster has to go through much more practice than a fly caster. As proof we can refer again to a popular citation—that the best fly casters take a long time in becoming proficient in the artistry of thumbing a multiplying reel and dropping the lure exactly where wanted, while a bait caster acquires skill in fly casting in a few hours.

While speaking of rods we dwelt a good deal

on the subject of different actions. A tyro will only delay progress by not having his rod balanced up with the right line. If the line is too heavy or too light, it will prove a serious handicap. Get your dealer or angling friend to see it first and say whether it is the right line. As soon as he indorses the outfit, you are ready to get going properly.

Let us advise against haste in acquiring accuracy or distance. Naturally, one craves instantly to be able to shoot a fly sixty feet or more because he wishes to be in a position to reach likely places, under stress of the compelling idea that the farther you cast, the more and bigger fish you catch. In theory it looks good, though often in practice the reverse happens. As in bait casting, accuracy counts more than distance. Distance can be achieved gradually, but when you try to do it before absorbing thoroughly the fundamentals you are only encouraging delay in acquiring proper form.

Soak your leader. Remember that now, and before you go to any fishing waters. The night previous to a visit to a stream have your leader box ready, the pads moistened, and place therein the leaders which you think you will use. Leaders are exceedingly brittle; they are hard to tie when dry or half dry, and crack instead.

You require neither a fly nor water to practice casting—just the rod, line and leader and a clean

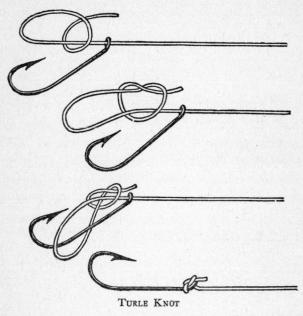

TURLE KNOT

bit of lawn that will not ruin a good fly line. Then remember these hints: Grasp your rod firmly in your right hand, if you are right-handed, with the reel under it. Place your elbow close to your body and hold it there all the while, however much

189

you realize that some great casters have a free movement which does not require the old Seth Green process of mastering the art at first by holding a book to the body while you are engaging in your work.

Another suggestion so that you will have no reason to start in the wrong manner: At no time let your rod tip go past vertical over your shoulder, or at the most, the fifteen degrees which the pull of your line accomplishes. If you do, it is going to defeat your object of making the right back cast for a perfect forward shoot.

Now strip out a few feet of line, whipping it back and forth. This is done by pulling the amount of line required from your reel with your left hand. Try to get out fifteen or twenty feet without changing the position of your arm. When you have that amount of line out on the lawn straight in front of you, with the rod tip necessarily pointing horizontally in the same direction, start slowly with an upward movement the pick-up of the line with your rod. Gradually, as the tip gets higher and higher, and almost at the point of half-way to vertical, give it a quick, short, upward jerk. Stop the movement of the rod entirely so that the tip will not pass back of your shoulder.

The instant you commence to feel the line straighten out back of you, bring the rod slowly forward and then, as the tip passes the shoulder in front of you, accelerate the act with a downward movement, and your line and leader will shoot out without any hitch or bellying. Do this over and over again until it becomes second nature; it can be accomplished without a single mishap. Then only are you ready to start increasing your distance and acquiring fly-fishing mastery.

Here are a few things to think about when you start to handle a fair amount of fly line. Before you commence to make the pick-up, get rid of all the slack line on the ground; strip it in with your left hand. It will take that much weight of line off the rod tip and save trying to lift what is unnecessary. Only when all the slack is out of your line will you be able to make a perfect pick-up. When on a stream try to pick up only the fly, not additional unnecessary line and water!

The next thing is to make that pick-up slow at the start, and give it impetus at the finish. Then the line goes back over your shoulder until the moment it is about to become inert or when it becomes inert through negligence. The forward cast ought to be effected just before the line straightens out entirely or when you begin to feel the pull. A novice is advised to wait until the pull, for fear he start his cast too soon, when the line is very likely to wrap around his neck. Obviously, if you wait until the line is dead behind you, it will fall to the ground. Try casting and looking back of you, on the recovery observing the flight of the line. This will teach you the reason for what has been written and in a very short while your casting will become automatically perfect because you will have discovered what is known as timing the period of duration for the line to travel back. Then your movements will soon synchronize with the amount of line you are trying to handle.

Often you will note that some known experts suddenly seem dispossessed for a time, when they pick up a new rod, of their skilled casting ability. It is not that they have suddenly lost their mastery but that they are not yet conversant with the necessary timing with the unfamiliar rod. Rods differ; some are faster than others and necessarily the amount of timing required with them varies.

When you change your place for practicing to water you will discover everything in actual fly casting much easier, particularly if you have sufficient room for the use of a long line. Always the advice offered to beginners by experts is to guard against not having enough room behind them for a backcast. And yet those who advise this hardly go on a fishing trip without hanging a fly or two in a tree!

Game fish are wary; they may respond to hooked, feathered creations which are made up to resemble the things upon which they feed, but, if they are presented awkwardly and with any disturbance, they will ignore them. This brings about advice on the subject of making the fly light noiselessly on the water like a daring winged insect. Therefore, we may readily observe that a fish will most times take fright if the line hits the water before the fly. We have said nothing about this while conveying the simple rudiments of fly casting, through fear that too much at once would bewilder the beginner.

Now start casting as formerly and, when your fly is a few feet from the water and your rod at an angle of about forty-five degrees, impart to your rod just a slight pull-back and at once your leader will straighten out, the fly touch the water properly and, when the line drops, it will not create any disturbance whatever. But it is well to master this before fishing, since it will insure more rises from game fish.

Casting the curve is about the same thing, though quite a bit of paper has been used by angling writers to instruct tyros. A little more lift or pull-back, as your fly begins to drop on the water, will cause it to fall quietly with quite a curve to the line and leader. The object of this may be readily understood the first time it is accomplished. If the entire line and leader straighten out immediately in downstream fishing, the fly does not behave like a natural insect. The pull of the current is instant. But with the curve the fly swings naturally toward the lair of the game fish with a more perfect representation of a living, downy insect.

Dry-fly fishing came to us from Britain and in the short time since its advent has become exceedingly popular. The art of dry-fly casting is very simple, yet is reputed to be something only the few can perform. Why people have come to believe that it requires extra skill I cannot quite ascertain. Perhaps it is due to the fact that when dry-fly fishing found its way to this side, it was taken up only by the rich; and the masses of fly casters, on account of ignorance of the expense of the equipment, never dreamed that it would be so easy for them to get in the game.

One of the most perfect dry-fly casters I ever saw was a Yiddish newsboy who used to watch tournament casters. He procured a cheap second hand outfit and began practicing in a park. His skill of manipulation was amazing, yet up to the time I saw him he had never been able to go fishing where he could put into practice his uncanny art. The poorest dry-fly casters I have ever seen were so-called expert dry-fly anglers. Their form was abominable, though the average wet-fly artist could have taught them proper form in a few minutes.

Dry-fly casting, as practiced almost everywhere in the United States, is nothing more than making a few false casts in the air above where the fish stay and then dropping the fly gently so it will float with no line pull on it. We do not use the same method of dry-fly casting as they do abroad. There they cast to the rise of a fish, stalking the slow streams to discover it, and, when they do, only fishing upstream in accordance with the standard, dry-fly method. The false casts are made to keep the fly dry. That is where most of the rod strain occurs. The fly has an ointment of paraffin applied to it to help its floating qualities. American and a few British fly tiers are adding more to the bodies and no ointment is necessary, particularly so with the cork-bodied ones.

When Americans go in for any sport, they do it pretty strenuously, and adapt their methods of pursuing the sport to local conditions. Therefore, they have enlarged dry-fly activities because their streams are different from those of our English cousins. Accordingly they fish lakes dry fly; they fish fast waters upstream and downstream dry fly, and, apparently, they enjoy it to the utmost, whether they rise any fish or not.

After you can cast according to instructions, consider yourself able to cast according to any method that fishing exigencies suggest, with only a little practice. Without attaching the old names, when you have to do side-casting to get your fly under the limbs of trees or hanging banks, about the only thing you have to think about is to change your style of holding the rod to horizontally, and proceed just as before, not permitting your rod tip to go too far back on the retrieve. This is a very easy way if you will hold your elbow against your side.

Quite a bit of line can be handled near brush or trees if fishing warrants it and you have room overhead, though no room behind you for a back-cast. It is what is known as the steeple cast. Pick up your line quickly and fling it with a motion which will bring it straight up high and almost over your head. Before the fly gets where it appears to be directed, come down with your rod, applying considerable force. You will be surprised to see how easily the cast is effected without endangering lodgment of the fly in brush or trees behind you. By stripping line and letting the loose line drop near your feet, you can strip, cast, and then shoot, in the above manner, all your loose line, releasing it from your left hand just at the instant you impart most power to the rod.

When you begin to aspire to distance casting, you must remember that it is not much else but shooting a good deal of loose line carried out by the power of the rod and the weight of the line already in motion before. It will be easy if you have a rod of sufficient power, because already you will have discovered that in fishing it is easier to cast a goodly amount of a line than a short amount. Your style of casting must be varied slightly, and, at the same time, you are to make use of the muscles in your forearm.

Start a slow pick-up, getting rid of all your slack line as before, and make your backcast. Bring your rod up until it is almost a foot higher than your head, your left hand following high with it; then, as you make the forward cast with a strong forward thrust of the forearm, the left hand follows and releases the line just as you make the shoot. In distance casting, you will observe that you will be able to pick up far more line easily if you point your rod tip directly in front of you and exceedingly low when you commence your retrieve.

This much is to be commented upon about casting great lengths of fly line: there is a limit to its value, though it is a pretty spectacle. With too much line out it is next to impossible to strike a fish. When you happen to hook one and it sticks on, rest assured it was not done by your efforts, but through good fortune alone.

There is another exceedingly good method of fly fishing when in close quarters with brush or trees behind you to interfere with the backcast. Start the pick-up as in your first lesson, but, instead of making the movement to bring the fly back of your right shoulder, start as though to bring it over your left shoulder; before completing the movement, change your motion and cast straight ahead from your right side as previously. Practice this and learn the proper timing. Then you will be amazed at how easily it handles a fair amount of line where there is not much room.

CHAPTER V

FLY CASTING FOR TROUT

A BRIEF essay on wading invariably has its place in the category of angling suggestions. Very little is written on the subject, though its importance is paramount. As far as catching trout is concerned, knowledge of wading properly is just as necessary as delicate artful casting; in fact, by the way an angler deports himself in a trout stream you can quickly judge his class, as well as, most times, correctly forecast his results. Now and then the blundering, careless, noisy, indifferent wader will take a large trout. Nevertheless, this must be attributed to luck and not to either skill or evidence of caution on his part.

Usually the novice tries to see how much fishing territory he can cover in a day on a stream, when it would be better to see how carefully and thoughtfully he could cover it. Haste results only in frightened fish and empty, or nearly empty, creels. You cannot fish skillfully and, at the same time, cover a great amount of fishing water in the right manner, whether you are wading or following along the bank.

There are some anglers who cannot get away from the fear of wading. They are afraid of water of even insignificant depth, and will stroll up and down a stream seeking for possible spots from which to make their feathered offerings, though they may be overlooking ideal parts and causing disturbances at every step to the trout hidden close to, or under the banks. Caution can well be exercised on the banks, for a vibration of apparently unnoticeable nature is easily transmitted to the speckled quarry.

Naturally, most wading is done downstream. Then it is easy to frighten trout. Since man has pursued them with so many different means they are always on the alert. Their wariness leads them to draw conclusions from even the slightest variation of their element. The wader usually stirs up gravel, sediment, sand or dirt, even dust and trash from limbs and brush against which his body happens to rub—all of which is carried downstream in advance, notifying the denizens of the water of an unusual presence above. Present a fly under these conditions and it is not reasonable to expect a rise. Wait until the water has become normal again, then a perfect cast is bound to produce a fish that is waiting in expectation of such an insect as your inanimate offering is supposed to represent.

A good wader surveys everything in front of him cautiously, trying to avoid every likely possibility of committing a *faux pas* that will alarm his quarry. Every effort to the contrary, some announcements are carried down from the bed of the stream. Nevertheless, an angler can be on his guard against stumbling and slipping by being thoroughly imbued with the idea that it is far better to fish carefully only a small distance in a day than it is to cover an extensive mileage. The man of haste unwittingly overlooks parts which ought to be productive, his lack of patience perpetually causing poor casting or casting at random instead of placing the tiny lure where the trout ought to be.

Obviously fish in running water take less fright from an angler's approach upstream. They watch for danger, rest and wait for food with their heads upstream. It requires no great amount of intelligence to understand why fishermen wading downstream cannot exert too great pains to conceal their movements; one deft, accurate cast, even though only occasionally executed, can be depended upon to bring more trout than a hundred indifferent casts. Notwithstanding, luck enters into the sport.

Fishing upstream is really very awkward work when the current is strong all along the route. The water taxes your leg- and body-strength, while the casting is not easy, as the incessant picking up of the fly spares neither the wrist, arm nor eyes. But it is done in wet-fly fishing, and sometimes dry-fly fishing in the United States is accomplished on streams not destined for that purpose, though the dry fly frequently becomes a wet fly, all precautions to the contrary. The likelihood of a large trout connecting is an irresistible urge, yet it takes a quick, masterful wrist to strike trout frequently in wild rushing water when you are persistently or occasionally casting upstream.

In upstream fishing, when casting spots are not always ahead, you will find a pleasant variation in shooting the fly to the likely parts amidstream, or, if you can wade to the center, to both banks. Then you may let the fly drift with no fear, if you are not in haste, of its floating to your feet.

Quiet, slow streams should be always cast upstream. This is most effective, either with dry or wet millinery. Do not try to get out too much line when dry-fly fishing. Many times streams which will bring no rises to the artistry of the most expert wet-fly caster during low water stages in summer weather suddenly produce attention on the part of trout to the tiny floaters.

Some people often wonder why dry-fly fishing has taken such a hold on the American angling public. I personally believe that it is not the newness of the sport, the necessary craftsmanship, nor assurance that it is the best method, but instead the love of all for seeing a game fish rise to the surface.

In dry-fly fishing work all possible parts of your waters, the logs, the rocks, the banks as close beneath the overhanging trees and shrubbery as possible. Remember the shadows, the little cascades at the foot of the falls. Whip them all consistently and carefully, above and below them. As a rift of current flows over gravel and subsides in a quiet pool, cast in the swift water just above so that the fly will float down naturally. Yet, as in all dry-fly casting, exercise caution to keep your fly afloat and prevent any possible dragging of line which might aid in immersing the fly.

204

With many a wet fly that I fish, in so far as I make false casts not to cause dryness on the part of the feather enticer, I try to create a shadow, like that of a most lazy, drowsing insect, believing that it has much to do with starting recalcitrant brook, brown and rainbow trout, otherwise suspicious or only dormantly receptive. I am particularly fond of casting the little cork-bodied trout midgets, that are nothing else but reduced patterns of bass bugs. They float perfectly, and yet I make false casts with them to create the impression in a trout's mind of a hovering insect so careless that it will become a part of that day's menu if he only waits alertly for it to dip a little closer to the flow.

The dictum of the anglers to fish during the hatching of the insects is reliability itself, when you have faith in it; follow it, and when it does not yield, try other methods. Fish come to flies best, is the universal declaration, when the hatch is on and they are on the surface extending gauzy, indolent wings for the sun to perform its drying process, and yet we catch big fellows at times with the wet flies.

My rule, that I follow almost everywhere, is to fish shallow streams à la dry fly, and deep waters wet, except lakes. Such a rule quite frequently has to be altered when I imagine a new stream has been made to order for the exact manner in which I decide to fish. And old streams, too, not infrequently effect a variation in my mode of casting.

We have never been able to tell truthfully from experience what time of day a stream ought to be fished while the insect hatching is on. Cold waters often do not produce such a situation until the sun is warm and at its zenith. The average angler will laugh at the idea of fishing at the noon hour, particularly on a clear day. If it happens to be cloudy, he subdues his tendency to ridicule and commences to cast.

There is a good deal to fishing with the clouds, those floating ones that are mingled momentarily with sporadic duration of sunlight, for, strange to say, often trout will rise vigorously when they appear thus, and become obdurate about rising as soon as they disappear. Still, in many waters trout are known to do good striking during a clear, cloudless day, and to cease when evening approaches. It is all a part of the anomalous lure of fly-fishing—never being able to foretell accurately what some streams will do, although by following general rules you will be likely to have success.

I have seen some famous brook and rainbow trout waters in the North that were not recommended by fly casters. They had tried them persistently without being able to lure the denizens. Some of the brown waters lack sufficient clarity for an angler to see fish in ordinary depth. When no responses came to their flies, they were not only disappointed, but stubbornly convinced that no trout existed there—or if there were any there, they were too small and too few to warrant any further notice. Yet their possibilities are not to be disregarded. The fish are not insect feeders, either because few insects hatch in those waters, or because minnows and small crustaceans are liked better.

I know of one rough stream spilling over the rocks and alternately forming brown pools in Quebec, near Ste. Marguerite, where I never saw the brook trout therein rise to the surface for an insect. They may do it, but I never saw them. Even the smallest fish I caught in these waters was gorged with tiny minnows. Seemingly with the abounding supply of these at hand, insects of all varieties were practically eschewed.

In the last reach of swift water on the lower Nipigon River, almost at the village itself, where brook trout are reputed to grow larger than any other place on the continent, I have fished regularly for a number of years. I have not only fished the stream, but also observed its peculiarities and irregularities with marked interest, because when I thought I had solved a rule without opportunities for variation, I discovered that there were many things I had yet to learn. In all that time, I have never seen brook trout over three pounds rise to insects nature produced on the clear, rapid, tossing flow. Yet I have taken trout there weighing up to eight and one-half pounds—brook trout—on flies. But they wanted large flies and seldom anything else, bass flies of patterns often different from the resemblance to any insect which I ever saw there.

I know of some waters where dry-fly fishing with the tiniest flies—sixteens—floating replicas of the natural insects—seems to be the only method for them. Always in dry-fly fishing the proper leader is necessary and I am partial to the fine tapered ones because they carry out excellently the main idea of the art, both as to casting and deceiving the trout. These streams conduct themselves in a manner so much the same that I am never prone to attempt to veer my program from that of former visits. They are fairly slow, shallow waters, and in summer produce browns and rainbows late in the evening.

Versatility ought to be regarded as the leading feature in the repertoire of the average fly caster. Fish the middle of swift rivers among the big rocks when trout are not attentive close to shore amidst the usually likely places. White water in such instances offers an opportunity, yet many anglers decide against it, although the Indians of the North Country invariably advise disciples of Izaak Walton never to neglect large submerged rocks, however swift or white the water racing above them.

Trout frequently puzzle me more than bass. I can never overcome the doubt I have in certain ideas I have absorbed from daily angling experiences. I expect them to be reversed when I rely on them most as certitudes. There was a pretty fair-sized brook trout in the Jackfish River that I wanted to connect with. He hid beneath a log jam which was miraculously suspended from a high bank like a roof. It was shallow, fairly clear,

though brown, gravel-strewn water. The fish saw
me and I saw him. I had hooked him and lost
him quickly afterward as I let him run toward a
tiny fall below. Again I saw him when he returned close to a small, peeled, submerged spruce
log under the jam. Evidently he saw me on the
gravel bar from which I was again offering him
feathered inducements, and he instinctively disregarded all my flies.

Then I went above him, actually climbed the
roof of his abode, the log jam, to get below, cast
awhile and resume my attentions. A cork-bodied,
closed-winged fly on a No. 6 hook, tied to resemble a Professor, dropped out of my hat band,
though I thought I had affixed it there securely.
The very moment it dropped on the water, that
big, red-spotted, alert warrior rushed for it. The
last I saw of him was a shimmer of silver and red
flouncing back toward the pool below.

I repeat that versatility ought to be a feature
in an angler's stock of tricks because personal experiences tell me it is actually out of the standard
accepted rut. I believe that lots of flies the exact
opposite of the insects to which they are rising
are occasionally worth more than passing notice.
What a trout is eagerly feeding upon irrefutably

seems what ought to attract them most, as well as cause least suspicion on their part.

I recall a hatching late one evening on a noted trout water. The trout were rising fast and furiously to a brown-winged, brown-bodied hatching. The disturbances on the surface were so frequent and numerous that it did not seem possible that I could avoid touching a fish had I wished it. With replicas I tried—every possible size—and not one gullible trout thought enough of them to rise. When all failed, I resorted to the greatest contrast I could find in my fly book. My first cast took a four-pounder. And I took two more later. Was it curiosity that brought the unlooked-for strike at the overgaudy large Wickham's Fancy, or merely anger that such an extraordinary looking object should intrude during the feast on the brown-winged insects?

Select a spot of quiet water in which to land your trout, if possible. Don't try to rough him upstream, nor hurry the valiant warrior. If you do, you are losing half the pastime. A well-hooked, big trout is worth a long engagement, and he will stand lots of rod straining while you maneuver to bring him away from rocks, logs and other impediments to your landing net.

CHAPTER VI

FLY CASTING FOR BASS

THE popularity of fly casting for bass has arrived in recent years. There was a time when anglers had the idea that bass rose to flies in some waters and in others they did not. Probably the cause of this belief was failing to note the peculiarities of many waters that were not fished with deceitful flies at timely moments; and because bass went strong for worms and minnows anglers used them as they did not wish to go home without fish. Then the purists saw so many using spinners as an added attraction that they hastily concluded that such a thing as angling for the bronze backs with flies brought only little success.

The failure of bass to become as popular as they should in early days of fly fishing was due to the flies made for the sport. Nearly all were enlarged trout patterns, no attention having been given to insects which bass favored. Bass bugs and feather minnows and carefully tied hair flies altered the entire list of flies for bass and styles of fishing. When bass bugs appeared many trout fishermen saw for the first time the fighting qualities of bass, but what most amazed and lured them into bass fishing was the never-to-be-forgotten rise of a bass to a floating bug. All the game fish for which they had angled had never displayed such characteristics of flinging themselves at a fly with wicked abandon, and then often following it with a cupping leap above water and subsequent quick dash beneath with marvelous rapidity.

The most expert trout angler discovered he had to learn to strike them with great celerity, for they were remarkably apt at ejecting the deceits, quicker, in fact, than most believed possible. What occurred between an angler and a vigorous bass after it was hooked was nothing more than an enduring battle with a most versatile fish.

It was difficult to calculate what a bass would do to achieve its freedom. The flights above water were so vigorous that the hook was ejected easily, or simply tore its way out of a bass' mouth. Then the category of the tricks employed by a small-mouth bass, or its less gamy cousin, the large mouth, was a mighty versatile one. One moment they were fighting on the surface, and then, before the angler thought they would vary such a plan, they were boring for deep water, winding spirally or in straight dashes, continually tugging at the line and evidencing a disposition to take advantage of an opportunity for their freedom by darting under logs, under and around rocks, weeds, sunken tree tops, and many other things which pester the life of an angler. Actually they seemed to be born with information of where each was, its value for their safety.

In swift water, a small-mouth bass, besides leaping and racing almost every way, displays another method of parting from the angler's inhibitive bit of steel. When all the battle seemed against them, practically all hope disappeared, they lay perversely against the current, crosswise, permitting the rapid flow to rush against their powerful broad bodies. The fly caster had then weight of water and fish to militate against his tactics while the truculent fish persisted. It was impossible, or too gruellingly wearisome to reel the quarry upstream; therefore, downstream the angler had to go in the expectancy of discovering a calmer locality, only to find out, often, that the fish had recovered strength and once more launched into a series of desperate efforts to regain its freedom.

In many waters fly casters persist in using tiny spinners attached to the eyed feather flies. The extra flash often helps to bring the bass to an attack when they are adverse to charging for the ordinary fly only. The spinners should be of the smallest size, and, while not moved too quickly, always should be kept revolving. You will save your rod by using only the smallest spinners, and get just as many fish. Stop the spinner as you bring it to the surface and only then make the pickup for the backcast; thus you will be relieved of lifting against unnecessary water resistance.

Using spinners is not to be recommended for upstream fishing. They will stop revolving as they do in bait casting. If cast straight against quick water, and they are not moving, they are no attraction to fish, though an expert can select little upstream currents and eddies, taking advantage of them very opportunely.

During the writer's early experience in fly casting for bass, he discovered when fish are most in the mood for flies with spinners attached or for flies unassisted by flashing metallic trimmings. He used as a dropper an ordinary fly and the trailer fly had a spinner connected. Invariably the bass proved which they wanted more; then the proper lure could be featured in the consequent fishing itinerary, for I had observed that in clear water there were many days when bronze-backs were actually frightened by the flash or mere disturbance of a spinner.

If wading mountain and other streams, you cannot be too careful. You will find bass more wary of a wader and his slightest disturbances than a trout. And this fish will not permit the close approach of a human. In shallow water, when something unusual disturbs them, they are instantly likely to dash for deep water and, unlike trout, once they see you, although they have catapulted themselves at your lure, it will be a useless thing to try to coax them into a rise again: yet they will go farther to seize a fly when actuated by some purpose than any other fish in existence.

In swift, clear waters, work downstream if possible when wading or working from a boat toward the bank. Do not try to give the standard fly any action; let the current do this, casting with

216

a curve, making the final part of the recovery as the line straightens out with a jerky movement. Watch the logs, banks, rocks, and the dark spots on shoals. The foot of falls is always an ideal place, and often white water copiously strewn with rocks produces nice fish, or they are likely to be found in still water close to the bank.

Casting a fairly long line is a great help in fly fishing for bass in big shallows, wide rivers or on lakes. Very often, early in the morning or late in the evening, both large-mouth and small-mouth bass of large poundage frequent shallows for minnows where there is very little opportunity for concealment. The value of long, quiet casting then may readily be seen. In casting lakes or slow streams with the ordinary flies let them sink quite a way before making recovery. Retrieve them in a jerky fashion, rather in a side-to-side movement, but be sure to cast with the wind.

In clear, swift water small flies are required. They are more likely to attract wise old bass; nevertheless, they present one disadvantage, the small hooks cut their way out during a rough engagement.

As on lakes, the large bass bugs, feather min-

217

nows and different kinds of hair flies of the floating variety always should be cast with the wind.
Observe the insects; note how they become spent
and the manner in which they fall on the water
and it will give you the right casting form for
bugs. Drop the bug on the water without any
splash of line, then let it rest a moment, just like
a bug when first its outstretched wings become
wet. A weary bass will look for imperfections of
movement such as the tyro invariably effects. But
a little skipping action is permissible as you start
recovery. When you see or hear a bass come for
this sort of lure, strike immediately; do not wait,
or the bass will fling it from its mouth faster than
you can visualize the act.

Remember to use a stiff rod for bugs; you will
need it to cast, also to turn fish from threatening
rocks, brush, logs and weeds. Rest assured bass
will try for them and tax your skill to the limit.
You need fairly strong leaders, too.

If you experience trouble in casting bass bugs
and feather minnows, recall the great amount of
air resistance the bodies and wings create. Do
not be in too great hurry, but be sure to get all
the slack out of your line with your left hand as
you start the recovery, picking up the bug grace-

fully and giving the line plenty of time on the backcast to stretch out sufficiently for the forward movement. If you do not, your cast will be an indifferent one.

In swift water, if you cannot cast sufficient distance, float the fly down to the fish by stripping out the necessary amount of line with your left hand. A more killing method than the following is hard to conceive. Place your fly on a leaf and let it float down to the desired spot; then, on its arrival there, jerk it off and watch out for the brawling bronze back near by to appear.

This can be done almost as successfully by letting it drift with the wind on a lake or slow stream. When there is a slight wind on the lake or a rippling breeze, if in the daytime, your chances for rising bass are excellent, for the bugs and similar fly-rod lures get the exact action necessary to attract fish without any need of manipulating a rod.

Late in the evening, after dark, or very early in the morning are the best periods for casting for large- and small-mouth bass on lakes or slow rivers. When the fish comes strike quickly, and at the same time exercise all your perceptive faculties to decide your forthcoming maneuvers, and the ultimate place to land your spent fish, as well as keep it from dangerous things which will aid it in escaping from the hook.

CHAPTER VII

TROUT FLIES AND FLY-ROD LURES

ARCHAIC is the opinion of many novices when they think that a list of flies presents a vast array of formidable mysteries understood only by those who have studied intensely the category of deceits for nearly a lifetime. Names apparently mean nothing to them, except, perhaps, to add to the mysticism of fly lore. Colors, too, while having a marked fascination, are hard for them to translate into what they ought to have for their supply before they have a sufficiently large, vital assortment to meet the noteworthy emergencies of bass and trout fishing. A color plate of the leading flies compels admiration, as well as a desire to possess all of them. In this they cannot go wrong, for the greater the number and variety of sizes proportionate are the chances of selecting one fly which will excite the fancy of the sly denizens of difficult waters.

There is still a tendency among old-timers, and some beginners, to look abroad for their supply of flies. Tradition exists that they surpass those made in this country, which is now by no means a fact. There are good English flies, good Scotch flies, good American flies, and badly made ones, on account of the necessarily cheap price at which they must be sold, coming from the same places. I favor the American-made flies because they are just as good as those made abroad, and chiefly, too, on account of their being made for American waters, and through study of American waters. I offer this without a desire to criticize exotic products of the fly-tying craft. Furthermore, the versatility of American fly tiers has held them to no fixed patterns; instead the desire to coöperate with anglers in providing them with their own discoveries seemingly transcends the more profitable routine of tying only certain standard patterns.

American fly tiers have learned a lot from the English regarding their craft, so that ultimately, through their observations of fishing and fishing conditions pertaining to our waters, they have been able to enlarge their lists, as well as vary contour and colorations of innumerable valuable feathered deceits. Here are lists of dry and wet flies for different waters, early, late and midseason. Do not stint yourself while making a selection. A well filled fly book invariably supplies the proper method of tempting fish.

POPULAR TROUT FLY PATTERNS

Abbey
Alder
Alexandria
Ashey
August Dun

Babcock
Bannock Chief
Beatrice
Beauty
Beaverkill
Bee
Bennet
Benny
Black Ant
Black Caddis
Black Freak
Black Gnat (male)
Black Gnat (female)
Black Hackle
Black Hackle—
  Silver Body
Black Palmer
Black Prince
Black Quill
Black Spider
Blue Spider
Blue Bee

Blue Bottle
Blue Dun
Blue Jay
Blue Quill
Blue Upright
Bowman
Bright Fox
Brown Alder
Brown Ant
Brown Drake
Brown Freak
Brown Hackle—
  Brown
Brown Hackle—
  Peacock
Brown Hackle—
  Red
Brown Hackle—
  Yellow
Brown Moth
Brown Palmer
Brown Sedge
Brown Spinner
Brown Stone
Buff Coachman
Bumble Bee

Caddis
Cahill

California Coach-
  man
California Royal
  Coachman
California Hackle
Caperer
Captain
Captain Scott
Carson
Carter Harrison
Catoodle Bug
Catskill
Cheney
Chippy
Cinnamon
Cinnamon Sedge
Cisco Fly
Claret Quill
Coachman
Coochy—
  Bonddu
Collins
Colonel Fuller
Cow Dung

Daniels Coachman
Dark Alder
Dark Caddis
Dark Coachman

223

POPULAR TROUT FLY PATTERNS—*Continued*

Dark Cow Dung
Dark Helgramite
Dead Chicken
Deer Fly
DeMille
Doctor Breck
Dr. Johnson
Dolly Varden
Dun and Gold
Dun and Silver
Dusty Miller

Emerald Dun
Emerald Gnat
Emmet
English Admiral
English Coachman
English Royal
  Coachman
Epting
Evening Dun

Ferguson
Fisher
Flight's Fancy
Flying Caddis
Forked Tail
Furnace Hackle

Gilt Coachman
Ginger Palmer
Ginger Quill
Gogebic
Good Night

Golden Spinner
Gold Ribbed Hares
  Ear
Governor
Governor Alvord
Governor Red Tip
Grasshopper
Gravel Bed
Great Dun
Green Drake
Greenwell's Glory
Grey Drake
Grey Dun
Grey Freak
Grey Hackle—
  Peacock
Grey Hackle—
  Red Body
Grey Hackle
  Silver Body
Grey Hackle
  Yellow Body
Grey Miller
Grey Monkey
Grey Palmer
Grey Quill
Grizzly Hackle
Grizzly King
Gunnison

Haley Hackle
Hardy's Favorite
Hares Ear
Heather Moth

Helgramite
Hemsworth
Henshall
Horse Fly
House Fly

Ibis
Ibis and White
Ibis Split
Idaho
Imbrie
Improved Gover-
  nor

Jamisons McGinty
Jenny Lind
Jennie Spinner
Jock Scott
Josephine
Jungle Cock
Juno

Kamloops
Katydid
Kimbridge Sedge
King of Waters
King of Fisher
Kitson

Lake Edward
Lake George
Laramie Spinner
Last Chance

POPULAR TROUT FLY PATTERNS—*Continued*

Lead Wing Coachman
Light Caddis
Light CowDung
Light Fox
Light March Brown
Light Montreal
Light Olive Quill
Little Marryat
Logan
Lord Baltimore
Lutz Favorite

Major Pitcher
Manchester
March Brown
McGinty
McKenzie
Mead
Mershon
Minehole
Montreal
Montreal White Tip
Mormon Girl
Mosquito

Newville
Nez-Perce

Oak Fly
Olive Dun
Olive Gnat

Olive Quill
Onondago
Orange Coachman
Orange Quill
Oriole
Pale Evening Dun
Pale Watery Dun
Parmacheene Beau
Parmacheene Belle
Peshtigo
Phil Mitchel
Pink Lady
Polka
Professor
Professor Blue Body

Queen
Queen of Waters
Quill Cahill
Quill Gordon

Rail Bird
Raven
Red Ant
Red Fox
Red Hackle
Red Palmer
Red Quill
Red Spinner
Red Tag Palmer
Red Upright
Reuben Wood
Richter's Special

Rio Grande King
Royal Coachman

St. Patrick
Salmon Fly
Sand Fly
Sassy Cat
Seth Green
Shad
Shoemaker
Shoshone Chief
Silver Blue Dun
Silver Doctor
Silver Monkey
Soldier Palmer
Soule
Special Black Ant
Special Red Ant
Spent Gnat
Spider
Split Ibis
Starling
Stone Fly

Tipperlinn
Tomah Jo
Trout Fin Fly
Trude
Turkey Brown

Upton's Fancy

Van Sant

Wickham's Fancy

POPULAR TROUT FLY PATTERNS—*Continued*

Western Bee
Whirling Blue
  Dun
Whirling Dun
White Freak
White Hackle

White Miller
White Moth
While Palmer
Willow
Woodcock
Wood Duck

Yellow May
Yellow Quill
Yellow Sally

Zulu

POPULAR DRY FLY PATTERNS

Beaverkill
Black Quill
Blue Bottle
Blue Dun
Blue Quill
Brown Hackle
  Peacock
Brown Hackle—
  Red
Brown Hackle—
  Yellow
Brown Palmer

Caddis
Cahill
Coachman
Cow Dung

Dusty Miller

Evening Dun

Flight's Fancy
Flying Caddis

Ginger Quill
Governor
Grey Hackle—
  Peacock
Grey Quill
Grizzly King

Hardy's Favorite
Hares Ear

Ibis

Jock Scott
Jungle Cock

Light Caddis

Major Pitcher
March Brown
McGinty
Montreal
Mosquito

Olive Dun
Olive Quill

Pale Evening Dun
Parmacheene Belle
Professor

Queen of Waters
Quill Gordon

Red Ant
Red Quill
Red Upright
Reuben Wood
Royal Coachman

Seth Green
Silver Doctor
Special Black Ant
Special Red Ant
Stone Fly

Wickham's Fancy
Whirling Blue
  Dun
White Miller
Willow

Yellow May

The practice of using more than one fly for trout or bass fishing is going into the discard as fast as snelled flies. Modern anglers much prefer to tie eyed flies direct to their leaders. Once in a while, you see men using two flies, yet often they are different ones and regarded by the caster as the quickest means of discovering to which sort of flies the particular game fish is paying the most attention. Uninfluenced by this, those who still use two or three flies at once on a leader are inspired by a desire to take more than one fish occasionally at one cast. Nevertheless, two fish put up no more thrilling battle than one. They are constantly pulling against each other and only in fast water, where the current pulls them downstream, does it require more effort to effect their landing.

The snelled fly is becoming obsolete. Once an angler uses an eyed fly, he is a convert to it. It was a great deal of trouble to keep snells moistened; many precious flies were constantly put out of commission from trying to affix them to a leader before this was sufficiently attended to, with the result that they were unserviceable afterward. But when you use eyed flies for trout fishing, have a clipper for snipping off the extra gut after you have learned to tie them correctly in one of the various ways.

You will note that dry-fly fishing for trout has created new patterns not yet recognized by the old class of anglers. The upright wings and the slightly heavier bodies distinguish dry flies from the regular variety. They have to float; not only is this accomplished by means of the wing arrangement and paraffin-oil doping, but a body slightly larger than ordinary aids a great deal.

You have to decide from experience what size of trout flies is the best for you under certain conditions, whether you fish them wet or dry. Only by personal experience can you solve what your stream requires; if you have not on hand all sizes, you are likely to miss the exceedingly great fascination of experimenting to discover the right one for lots of fish.

When you are after the record-breaking brook trout, those running over three and four pounds, which are not infrequent in some northern waters, you must have patterns tied on hook sizes up to No. 1/o. This looks like a mighty big affair to the average fly caster for trout, who regards taking a nineteen-inch or twenty-inch trout as a great achievement. Some of the big boys absolutely demand big flies. Some of the successful anglers for trout of great poundage use entirely salmon and bass flies. I know of one who has annually caught a big share of large stream trout who fishes with nothing else but salmon flies and bass flies. He confines himself to Silver Doctor, Parmacheene Belle, Professor, Jock Scott and Babcock. When these will not produce, he quits fishing, and declares there is no use attempting for the while with any other patterns. Further, he has large bass bugs made in these patterns for the same purpose. But this must not be accepted as an inflexible rule that no large trout will take small flies. They do in some waters, and do not in others.

Present-day trout fishermen rely considerably on what are known as true-to-nature flies. The great majority of these are fished à la dry fly and are floaters. But the American and English varieties are exquisitely tied and represent a really high order of craftsmanship. Special boxes with compartments and books are made for them in order that they can retain their shape permanently. The English cork-bodied floaters have recognized value with trout fishermen. The cork-bodied floating midgets or trout bugs, which are made like bass bugs, although of much smaller proportions, are effective killers. They have a versatile feature, much appreciated, because they catch trout in nearly all waters, float always, and have no need of any dry fly oil applications.

The list of fly-rod lures for trout ranges from tiny spinners with flies attached, spinners in nickel, gold, silver, and copper finish without flies, trout-size feather minnows, every known bug, frogs and minnow made of rubber and other materials, to real, tiny, wooden plugs—exact reproductions in reduced size of the large bait-casting plugs used for bass and larger game fish. They are trout angling essentials. Very often they bring weighty rises when nothing else will arouse the activity of the denizens of brooks, streams and cold lakes. A little rod manipulation causes them to disport themselves exceedingly like real minnows.

All flies are now tied on barbless hooks, when requested. With these hooks an angler can free a small or large fish without injury. Returning to the water the undersized ones in good condition insures better fishing the following season.

CHAPTER VIII

BASS FLIES AND FLY-ROD LURES

WE are obliged once more to mention the fact that snelled and eyed bass flies for a time were solely standard trout patterns tied on much larger hooks. Even the various upright and reverse winged effects were both visioned and made with the trout patterns in mind, as well as developing weedless properties. Bass fishing enlarged the list. Experience created new patterns, though often we are pretty sure some patterns are not represented in nature; but the guiding idea came from the coloration or mingled coloration of some other sort of lure which was discovered to be arousing the striking propensities of bass.

Some will declare that bass are attracted only by a definite color or combination of colors. Other anglers will declare the contrary. Then along comes an exceedingly successful fisherman who will state that creations closely resembling the things of nature are what most bring large-

and small-mouth bass to rise to artificials, though it may create a fussy disturbance like the living insect.

The first users of anything resembling bass bugs of the present type were natives of the Saint Francis River in Arkansas. I should qualify this statement by saying, those within my knowledge. It was a long time before any appeared on the market in their present shape and dress. They had a large bottle cork which was tied on one or two long shanked hooks with various colored feathers—mostly those of turkey. Their art, which they designated as "spatting," consisted largely of attaching the lure to a long cane pole with a stout cord and flinging it with a big splash on the water. This attracted bass from amidst the smart weed, lily and flag beds to where there was open water, and they attacked the fussy looking combination promptly on beholding it. It was designed as a large-mouth bass lure. But all models and modifications of this gross fly had floating qualities and buglike appearances in their patterns.

The majority of eyed bass flies in standard patterns are fished with spinners attached. Yet many of the old veterans of the bass-fly fishing sport for no good reason attach unsportsmanlike principles to any one thinking of casting these flies with spinners in their presence. Bass will fight just as hard and just as long with the spinner connected as they will on the standard eyed flies without spinners. Spinner fishermen are almost as strong for various patterns of feathered and hair flies as other bass anglers. But after they use them for a long time, it is difficult for them to accommodate their art to regular angling à la purist. In the first place, they lack confidence in their flies, alone, and in the second, they have great difficulty in casting any fly sans their favorite spinners.

Potent are the innumerable hair flies or combined hair and feather flies. It would be flouting tradition even to hint that necessarily they have no place in an angler's fly book, and others serve as well. They are really attractive lures.

There are the floating varieties, which we will consider first. They are made of natural and dyed bucktail, skunk, squirrel-tail, badger and other hair, with large bodies, without and with streamers of rooster hackles, without and with wings or mere abbreviations. The big bodies are to assure floating properties. The hair flies in

233

most instances when on water or below the surface have an amazing insectlike crawl which certainly tantalizes fish. They should be dried by false casting and all the water shaken out of them before they are stowed away. A hair wing approximates very closely that of a living insect when it is stretched out flat on the water. When these flies are manipulated with a rod, they positively appear to flutter.

A lady angler who had never previously seen the winged bucktail bass flies remarked, when they were shown to her, that there was no sense whatever in trying to lure wily bronze backs with those comical little false mustaches. Her companion insisted that she try them, giving her good preparatory advice about granting more time to her backcast. Without faith she tried them late one evening and forthwith agreed that it was her banner fishing trip, for she landed seven bass averaging close to four pounds each, in a short time.

It is possible for an angler to have such an experience in certain fishing waters, so their assortment should not only be of varied colorations but in hook sizes from No. 8 to 1/0 and 2/0.

What influence the old cork body and feathers

of the Arkansas "spatters" had on the origin of the present-day bass bug is problematical. It suffices to say that the type used to-day was fished with in Tennessee a number of years before they claimed renown on the upper Mississippi River and then derived first the name of Mississippi River, or Callmac Bugs, the latter coming from a noted fly and bait caster who manfactured them, named Cal McCarthy. But in justice to the southern origin, the product of the South antedated by a number of years those seen on the upper Mississippi. In fact, briefly, the first true bass bugs were made to catch bream with a fly rod late in the evening and at night. Bass were seen to take them, and, accordingly, they were made larger.

An angler who fails to fish with bass bugs and a fly rod misses a whole lot. They are everyday and nearly all-season lures. When a bass really wants one he displays no hesitancy, but, instead, catapults his amazingly strong self at them with immeasurable speed and vigor. Such a spectacular leap! Such a wonderful subsequent battle! No fly-rod artifice surpasses these for night fishing. Fish with bugs and your striking form ultimately will become perfection itself.

You have to learn to strike immediately or go fishless.

Two models of bass bugs are made, and many patterns: flat wings, called Mississippi River patterns, and those with erect or upright wings. Fancy alone leads one to decide which is better, though those with flat wings are easier to cast than the upright winged article and do not muss up quite so quickly in the restricted compartments of an average fly box or fly book.

A cork body is shaped to resemble the body of some insect; this is split and, after the application of potent cement in the cleavage, it is tied on a non-slip hook. There are different patterns of non-slip, non-twist hooks and devices. The bodies are painted with high-grade enamel, then a dress on each side of bucktail for the legs, tail and wings. Such is an abbreviated description of the mode of making bass bugs.

Feather minnows might well be called the compatriots of bass bugs, for they have the cork body, yet get most of their attractiveness from the addition of rooster hackles—long streamers tied to present their individual terminations in the opposite direction, criss-crossing in order to convey the impression of a crippled minnow, or a minnow none too well possessed of all its perfect physical qualities. A feather minnow rolls, darts and dives according to fly-rod ministrations, and just what it ought to do leads into many complications, so we will only observe: try it, and you will get results on your favorite water and determine only then which is the best way to employ it.

Nature lures used in fly-fishing for bass call for bugs of shapes quite dissimilar from anything existing and they appear almost every year at the instigation of anglers who report big catches with them. Those most resembling the creations of nature are artificial grasshoppers, crickets, dragon flies, frogs, helgramites, mice and minnows. Rubber is used in some instances to make them, particularly the hopper, cricket and dragon fly, but cork, feathers and hair on the best balanced ones float well, and are tremendously fascinating. How effectively they bring rises can aptly be forecast if you once visualize the way, on numerous occasions, you have seen bass grab a dragon fly at all hours of the day.

Grasshoppers and crickets were dependable baits in their live form when you were a boy. The best of the artificials have no hard projections for legs, as a bass will eject such quickly before the hook can penetrate. Rubber helgramites are favorites of a great number of anglers, as well as other nature lures made from this material. As they are light, they are quite easy to cast.

The outfit of all fly-rod anglers for bass should include what are commonly called fly-rod lures. They are exact, small reproductions of bait-casting plugs made for angling with fly rods. Their resemblance to a minnow when in the water is remarkably true, in coloration and in action, too. But they demand a rod with plenty of backbone. One soon learns how to bring out their most attractive qualities, for they respond to the slightest movement of the wrist, diving and darting. When no action is given by the rod, they come to the surface and rest.

As the wooden fly-rod lures depend for their convincing action on the grooved or slanting shaped head encountering water resistance, naturally a slight rod strain is exerted which will ultimately put a bow in the best fly rod, unless the right kind of handling is given it. This, however, is simplicity itself. Before you make the pickup, stop all rod movement, then the little wooden deceit will come to the surface and float. While it is thus at rest, get rid of all slack line and make the pickup as ordinarily, and then water resistance of no sort will be encountered. If you do not follow these instructions, you will have to labor for the pickup and, at the same time, subject your nice rod to an unnecessary strain.

Weedless flies are frequently in order, and the absence of an assortment in a fly book is felt when you fish mossy waters, lily pads, weed beds, pockets in flags, rushes and similar growth. There the fish will resort, for they know they are well concealed in a formidable position to pounce on their prey. And they do not frequent such places a great deal unless an active feeding urge is on them. The weedless lures are absolutely necessary if you intend to fish these parts. If your bugs, flies, hoppers, crickets and dragon flies are not equipped with weedless devices, you will merely become entangled and catch trash instead of fish. Weed guards of light wire will not hinder casting, yet they will gather no extraneous matter. Moreover, some flies with reversed wings guard the hooks against such a contingency and still retain their luring powers.

A shortage of flies when on a fishing trip is

nothing but the detour road to losing opportunities. A good supply of known killers, floaters and wet flies is sure insurance against fishless hours.

POPULAR BASS FLY PATTERNS

Abbey
Alex Friend

Black Gnat
Black Hackle
Black Prince
Black Queen
Bob Davis
Brown Hackle
Brown Moth
Bucktail Red Tag

Carter Harrison
Chadwick's Sun
  beam
Clark's Fancy
Colonel Fuller
Cow Dung

Dennison
Dilg's Gem
Dr. Henshall

Ferguson
Fox Squirrel

Golden Spinner
Gray Goose

Gray Hackle
Gray Squirrel
Grizzly King
Guinea

Hadley's Choice
Henshall

Ibis
Ibis and White

Jacquin
Jenny Lind
Jock Scott
Jungle Cock

King of Waters

Lake George
Lord Baltimore

Manchester
McGinty
Montreal
Montreal, Dark
Montreal, White
  Tip

Orange Miller

Parmacheene
Parmacheene Belle
Peet's Favorite
Professor

Queen of Waters

Red Ibis
Reuben Wood
Royal Coachman

St. John's Pal
Sam Skinner
Seth Green
Silver Doctor
Split Ibis

White Miller
Wilder's Discovery

Yellow Drake
Yellow May
Yellow Sally

Zane Grey

CRAPPIE, BLUEGILLS AND PAN FISH

Not so many years ago on a swift stream a thought came to my mind when the bass were not striking that perhaps there were other means by which I could employ my idle time fishing, as well as improve my fly-fishing form. I thought awhile before mental manifestations appeared of the kind which would designate a direct, sensible, enjoyable effort. I decided to practice casting as long distance as possible, and ultimately see if there was any way to add to my ability to shoot more line than I was accustomed to laying out with a five and three-fourths ounce fly rod.

I began wading out in fairly swift water, with downstream as my objective, but changed my fly, substituting a small trout fly, March Brown, for the bass fly which I had tied to my leader. I did it only because it signified less air resistance, and would aid greatly in this distance thing which was now absorbing my attention. I shot out considerable line, then stripping out a greater amount, permitting the current to carry it downstream, to see if I could pick up greatly. This was the way the fly came to reach the calmer water, and sink. I was surprised to feel quite an energetic tug.

I struck, and, finding that it was impossible to pick up my line as customary, I began to reel in slack and ultimately discovered that I was hooked on to some sort of fighting fish, the kind I did not know until a few minutes later when I landed a large crappie.

Again I sent my fly down where the swift water terminated and permitted it to sink. Whereupon I had another strike, and responding with my rod quickly I connected with another crappie of the same size as the first. I realized that a new avenue of sport was opening, and did not quit until I had caught six of these fish.

While my experience had nothing in it to cause any one to believe that there were many fresh water fish other than bass that would rise to flies, because others had proved it time and again perhaps before my natal day arrived, still it made me commence to indulge, and I have many times afterward, when the most valuable game fish refused to strike any sort of lure, enjoyed myself exceedingly whipping for the little fellows. It encouraged trying for other fish. At the same time I gained marked knowledge on the subject of flies which would attract, then I was able to augment my opportunities.

242

It may amaze those who have not tried fishing for them to learn that often some varieties of sunfish, such as are known as red bellies and blue-gills, for their size put up just as hard a fight as a bass or any variety of trout. Then rock bass and the black-spotted, red-eyed chaps, known most everywhere as goggle eyes, can be taken with flies, if angled for properly.

The only time I do not advise changing from a regular bass fly rod to an exceedingly light trout rod for taking these small fish is when you are on a lake late in the evening and the expected captives are out on shoals and the water is so clear that it requires quite long-distance casting to tempt them. Often they are as shy as any other game fish, despite their apparent plenitude. You have to cast far to offer your fly to them tempt-ingly, for if they see you, they suddenly lose appetite for your best creations. It is too much of a tax on a nice delicate fly rod to cast long dis-tances continually with it. But when fish are close, as they will be in fairly deep water, a light whippy rod, and all else in the outfit to balance it prop-erly, simply enhances your sport.

In fairly deep water the small pan fish men-tioned above respond nicely to wet flies. Let them sink a bit before making recovery, and **if** there is one of these little fishes around it will soon let its presence be known. A number of experienced anglers add a small shot to their leader, just as they often do in early spring trout fishing, so the deceit will go down deep, and make phlegmatic fish come.

The addition of a tiny spinner does away with the necessity of shot on the leader, furthermore, it greatly accentuates the chances to lure fish. Do not use large spinners, but the tiniest ones obtainable, and there is no need of recovering them fast. I know one angler, who derives vast pleasure from specializing in the small pan fish, who is an ardent efficient advocate of spinners. He likes to fish most little brooks with rock-strewn beds. He wades downstream, permitting the lure to touch bottom before starting it into any action whatever. Then he reels ever so slowly or strips in his line with his hand so that the actual movement resembles a lazy minnow, moving indolently, rolling on its sides, and every once in a while creating a sort of flash like a miniature piece of polished silver. That his methods are correct are well borne out by achievement. He catches a nice creel full of these favorite fish while the writer, casting according to accepted rules sans spinners, obtains very little reward for his efforts.

The only time I am able to equal my friend who uses spinners in his beloved little red sunfish brooks is when instead of a fly or spinner I tie on to my leader one of the very small wooden lures, the replicas of bait-casting lures, about which we spoke a while back—the very smallest size, with hooks at the largest, No. 8 size. Only the most meager application of the rod tip will impart to it an excellent minnow mimicry, and no fish of the game variety in any sense of the word can resist it. But the attractiveness of this small wooden object is by no means limited to streams or small brooks; the denizens of the largest lakes will come rushing eagerly after it when they are in striking mood.

The wet fly on lakes and big rivers has a large number of advocates who go after the small pan fish, yet on the other hand, there are many dry-fly artists who do not consider it beneath their notice. Moreover, they realize most amazingly well that they can carry out true-to-nature ideas with marked success, and thereby learn a great deal about what sort of insect is most enticing to fish.

245

Sunfish and bluegills, as well as rock bass and goggle eyes, are very responsive to the food gifts of nature. They are particular at times, too, and, though often, like other game fish out of curiosity, belligerency and what not, they will seize something which does not in the least resemble anything designed by Providence, at certain times imitations must be very perfect to deceive them in the least. But their love for floaters is outstanding early in the morning or late in the evening when you behold them coming to the surface for insects.

You will surely get good results if you cast as you do in regular dry-fly fishing of the most æsthetic kind for trout. Another dry-fly method that always proves valuable is to cast with the wind to within a short distance of where you know the fish are feeding, and then stripping line, permit your dry trout fly to float to your target.

About as attractive a type of dry fly as you can find are the cork-bodied trout bugs and midgets of tiny size. They are obtainable in a sufficient variety of patterns so you can procure a selection which is bound to make the little fish take notice and come to them avidly. They have a very life-like action under the impulse of the slightest breeze, and then you are never required to manipulate your rod to make them start their luring saltatory act.

Of the numbers, with whom I am acquainted, in favor of fishing regularly for the favorite pan fish with fly rods, a majority prefer to do their work at night. They catch a lot and the best sizes, too, and most of them consider the cork-bodied bugs of small size the most potent for bringing rises during the dark hours. Their preference seems to be for nights that are very dark, neither moon nor star shining, and the only light they have by which to see is provided by the flashlights which they carry in their coats or trousers pockets. Some tell me that they then fish true-to-nature, by guessing what the fish are feeding upon, and ultimately being apprised by a strike after they try out a large assortment of flies. They are so convinced that this is the just-right method, that once they have a rise to a fly nothing will induce them to change for another.

There may be greater fascinations in the angling pastime than fishing for crappie, bluegills and sunfish, but no better filler-in for idle moments

247

when the recognized game fish are not on the rise, and the beloved element of the unexpected occurs frequently. It offers to many unlimited opportunities to improve their casting ability.

INDEX

249

INDEX

(1)